Prizefighting
The Age of Regency Boximania

Richard Humphries

JOHN FORD

Prizefighting

The Age of Regency Boximania

*The taste for pugilism extended
itself so generally of late years that
every one now felt its influence . . .
this was the era of Boximania . . .*
JON BEE in *Fancyana*, 1824

DAVID AND CHARLES : NEWTON ABBOT

ISBN o 7153 5325 X

Set in 11 on 13pt Plantin
and printed in Great Britain by
Latimer Trend & Company Limited Plymouth
for David & Charles (Publishers) Limited
South Devon House   Newton Abbot   Devon

Contents

Illustrations

7

Foreword

The true . . . material of the story is . . . the contrast between
the realities of the ring and the common romantic
glorification or sentimental abhorrence of it.

G. B. SHAW: *Cashel Byron's Profession*

The purpose of this book is to present one sport as a chapter in
the social history of what is conveniently called the Regency
period. I have attempted to explain the development of the sport
of prizefighting and its relation to the society in which it reached
its apogee. Rules and ritual brought some sort of order, even
refinement, to the rough instinctive activity of fighting; and these
rules and rituals, the language of the sport, the manners of its
heroes and supporters reflect the society in which they evolved.
We can understand the sport fully only by studying contemporary society, and an understanding of a sporting phenomenon
can perhaps throw light on areas of social history.

The prizefighters stand in a symbolic relation to the Regency
period and indeed pugilism became a fashion and even a cult.
The sport was patronised by royalty and the nobility; it excited
the imagination of writers from Dr Johnson to Hazlitt, Keats,
Clare, Tom Moore and Borrow. It provided a muse for the
graphic skills of such artists as Hoppner, Rowlandson and the
Cruikshanks. Lord Byron and George Morland revelled in the
company of pugilists and indulged themselves in sparring with
their cronies. Political figures, Windham and Althorp, could

neglect their other interests to watch a fight, never hesitating to moralise on the ethical values which a prizefight could inculcate. That conservative radical, William Cobbett, was equally persuaded of the manly virtues stimulated by boxing.

The public schools seemed veritable hotbeds of pugilism, for at Eton, Harrow, Westminster and Rugby the boys were devoted to the sport. But the greatest number of the Fancy, that collective noun for the followers of prizefighting, were the people whose schools are unrecorded, whose memoirs were never written and who never thought to rationalise their enthusiasm. The Johnny Raws in rural England and the millions who lived in the narrow rooms and dirty alleys of London and the new industrial towns, these were the men who made up the enormous crowds that thronged to every prizefight. The prizefighters themselves came from among such people and for the first time gentlemen took as their heroes scions of the lower classes. With the masses the popularity of the prizefighters was equalled only by that of such criminals as Dick Turpin and Jack Sheppard. Undereducated sub-literary readers cut their teeth on the pugilistic and criminal reports that formed the basis of such newspapers as the *Weekly Dispatch*, *Bell's Life*, and the promotions of the indefatigable journalist, Pierce Egan. There was a flood of cheap prints portraying the current heroes.

Pugilism made an impact in some unusual ways. John Keats' friends persuaded him to attend a fight between Randall and Martin at Crawley Downs to distract him from his overwhelming grief over the recent death of his brother Tom. (Lytton Strachey was to seek such a diversion from depression 100 years later.) The country poet, John Clare, in his madness believed himself to be a pugilist.

There are darker areas and the story of prizefighting is not one of unalloyed glamour. Jack Strong drowned himself in a fit of drunken depression, Little Gadzee succeeded in his second attempt at suicide and 'Bully' Hooper dragged himself to the workhouse to die. There were many, including such sportsmen as

Surtees and 'Nimrod', who opposed prizefighting on humanitarian and ethical grounds. There are clear connections between
the sport and the criminal underworld.

This book examines those darker areas, but it is neither a
criticism of prizefighting as a sport nor an apologia. It is a study
of the sport and its social setting and differs, therefore, from the
few previous histories by contemporary and later sporting journalists. Without, I hope, losing the excitement and glamour with
which the romantic novelists have ever invested it, I have tried to
ascertain and explain the factual record from the contemporary
newspapers, magazines, prints and memoirs.

Chronology of the Prizering

1787-1824

1787 18 January   Tom Johnson beats Bill Warr at Oakingham. General recognition of Johnson as Champion.

19 December   Johnson beats Michael Ryan at Wradisbury, Bucks.

Capt Topham, editorial director of *The World*, 1787–91.

1788 9 January   Richard Humphries beats Daniel Mendoza at Odiham, Hants.

9 June   John Jackson beats Tom Fewtrell near Croydon in presence of Prince of Wales. Gillray print.

August   Fatal ending to fight between Earl and Tyne at Brighton in presence of Prince of Wales.

Publication of *The Art of Manual Defence* and *Modern Manhood*.

1789 11 February   Johnson beats Ryan at Rickmansworth.

6 May   Mendoza beats Humphries at Stilton, Hants.

22 October   Johnson beats Isaac Perrins at Banbury.

1790 30 August Big Ben Brain fights draw with 'Bully' Hooper (protégé of 7th Earl Barrymore) at Newbury.

29 September Mendoza beats Humphries at Doncaster.

1791 17 January Ben Brain defeats Tom Johnson to become Champion. Ill-health prevents Brain from fighting again.

1792 14 May Mendoza beats Warr at Smitham Bottom and is recognised as Champion.

October First publication of *Sporting Magazine*, which completes a *History of Boxing* in five monthly parts.

1794 April Death of Big Ben Brain.

1795 15 April 'Gentleman' John Jackson beats Mendoza at Hornchurch to become Champion. Jackson retires from the ring.

1796-9 Comparative lull in promotion of major prizefights; the volume of newsprint and prints diminishes, but interest in the sport remains high and Mendoza, Warr and particularly John Jackson at 13 Bond Street, London, establish successful schools.

1797 22 August First fight at Moulsey Hurst (Jack Bartholomew v Tom Owen). Moulsey later to become most popular venue.

1800 A new hero, Jem Belcher, comes to London from Bristol and, after several successful fights, he beats Andrew Gamble at Wimbledon on 22 December and is acknowledged Champion.

1801 Belcher twice beats Jem Bourke.

1802 First benefit at the Fives Court in Little St Martin's Street. Sparring exhibitions continue here until the Court is demolished in a development project for Trafalgar Square early in 1826.

1803   24 July   Jem Belcher loses the sight of his right eye playing rackets.

1804   7 August   Dutch Sam beats Caleb Baldwin at Highgate.

1805   8 October   Henry Pearce (the 'Game Chicken') beats John Gully at Hailsham, Sussex, a fight watched by the Duke of Clarence.

6 December   Pearce beats Jem Belcher at Blythe, Notts, and becomes the Champion. Pearce is never able to defend his title, suffering from consumption, from which he dies in 1809.

1806   8 February   Dutch Sam beats Tom Belcher (brother of Jem) at Moulsey and is now recognised as Champion of the lightweights.

21 August   Dutch Sam again beats Tom Belcher, at Crawley Common.

1807   14 February   John Gully beats Bob Gregson at Newmarket and becomes Champion.

1808   10 May   Gully again beats Gregson, at Market Street, Herts. Gully retires.

25 October   Tom Cribb beats Gregson at Moulsey. Cribb now Champion.

1809   1 February   Cribb beats Jem Belcher at Epsom Downs.

1810   31 May   Dutch Sam beats Ben Medley at Moulsey.

10 December   Tom Cribb beats Tom Molyneux, the American negro, at Copthorne Common.

1811   30 July   Death of Jem Belcher.

28 September   Cribb beats Molyneux at Thistleton Gap. Cribb does not fight again but is known as the Champion until 1821.

2 December   Presentation of Silver Cup to Tom Cribb at Castle Tavern.

Pancratia by Bill Oxberry published.

1812   *Boxiana*, the first of the 'vade-mecums' to pugilism, by Pierce Egan, was published in parts.

1813   *Boxiana* published in book form.

1814   3 May   First fight in the Pugilistic Club ring (Bill Richmond v Davis the Navigator) at Coombe Wood.

22 May   First dinner of Pugilistic Club, Sir Henry Smith in the chair and Lord Yarmouth as speaker.

5 June   Pugilists spar before visiting Czar of Russia, King of Prussia and Generals Platoff and Blücher at Lord Lowther's house.

8 December   Bill Nosworthy beats Dutch Sam at Moulsey.

Tom Belcher becomes licensee of Castle Tavern, Holborn, succeeding Bob Gregson. Daffy Club formed at the Castle with Jemmy Soares as President.

1815   18 April   Lifeguardsman Shaw beats Tom Oliver at Hounslow. Shaw soon to be killed at Waterloo.

6 June   Jack Scroggins beats Nosworthy at Moulsey.

13 December   Dan Donnelly beats George Cooper at the Curragh, Kildare.

1816   4 October   Jack Carter beats Ned Painter at Gretna Green and claims to be the Champion, as Cribb has not fought for five years.

There were nine fights at Moulsey Hurst and ten at nearby Coombe Wood and Coombe Warren in this year.

Pierce Egan joins the *Weekly Dispatch* as sports writer.

1817   There were seven fights at Moulsey.

1818   1 April   Tom Spring (Cribb's protégé) beats Ned Painter at Mickleham Downs.

7 August   Painter beats Spring at Kingston.

5 December   Jack Randall beats Ned Turner at Crawley Downs and proves himself the greatest of the lightweights. This fight was watched by John Keats and by Tom Moore.

The second volume of *Boxiana* by Egan published and first volume reissued as 'Volume 1'.

1819   4 May   Randall beats Jack Martin at Crawley.

21 July   Dan Donnelly beats Tom Oliver at Crawley.

Publication of 'Tom Cribb's Memorial to Congress' by Tom Moore.

1820   28 February   First benefit at Royal Tennis Court in Gt Windmill Street, Haymarket, London.

May   *Blackwoods'* 'Luctus on the Death of Sir Dan Donnelly' (who had died on 18 February 1820).

17 July   Ned Painter beats Tom Oliver at North Walsham.

There were twelve fights at Moulsey Hurst this year.

Publication of poems under the title *The Fancy* by John Hamilton Reynolds, friend of Keats.

1821   20 February   Tom Spring beats Tom Oliver at Hayes.

19 July   Pugilists attend coronation of George IV as pages.

11 September   Randall beats Martin again at Crawley (this time in one round).

11 December   Bill Neat beats Tom Hickman (the 'Gasman') at Newbury. Neat now recognised by some as Champion.

Publication of third volume of *Boxiana* by Pierce Egan.

1822   January   Publication of first issue of *Annals of Sporting and Fancy Gazette* (edited by Jon Bee).

22 March   First issue of *Bell's Life in London*.

Publication of Hazlitt's essay 'The Fight' in *New Monthly Magazine*.

John Jackson presented with a service of plate worth £300 for his services to prizering.

1823   20 May   Tom Spring beats Bill Neat at Andover and is recognised as Champion.

Presentation of silver cup to Tom Spring.

There were eight fights at Moulsey in this year.

1824   7 January   Tom Spring beats John Langan at Worcester.

February   First issue of *Pierce Egan's Life in London and Sporting Guide*. Egan left the *Weekly Dispatch* in January 1824.

8 June   Spring again beats Langan near Colchester.

23 November   Tom Cannon beats Josh Hudson at Warwick for £500 a side.

Publication of Jon Bee's *Boxiana* (usually called volume 4).

This year represents a turning point in the history of the sport for (1) Tom Spring retired
  (2) John Jackson closed his rooms in Bond Street
  (3) Ned Neale and Jem Burns were prosecuted for fighting at Moulsey Hurst which virtually closed down Moulsey and caused many of the gentlemen fanciers to withdraw their patronage.

B

CHAPTER ONE

Introduction: Spring versus Langan

The first fight between Tom Spring and John Langan took place at Worcester Race Course on Wednesday, 7 January 1824. It was a long battle fought with skill and desperate courage, a classic contest of the scientific boxer against the hitter. The fight was watched by a huge crowd, which reflected the variety of English society from the Corinthian to the 'tag-rag and bob-tail'. The crowd, as we shall see, was to play a significant part in the progress of the fight. Spring was the Champion of England, Langan the Irish Champion, and, to the Fancy at least, it seemed that national honour was at stake.

Pierce Egan's description of the fight and its preliminaries serves as an introduction to the ritual of the prizefight at the end of pugilism's golden age. There could be no better guide to the

world of the prizefighters and the Fancy than Egan, the 'Plutarch
of the Prize Ring', most prescient of the Fancy, and a self-made
journalist with a style peculiarly suited to picture his colourful
and brutal subject.

It was on Thursday, October 23, 1823, at the Castle Tavern,
Holborn, that Tom Belcher, on the part of *Langan*, deposited £50
towards making a match for £300 a-side with SPRING. On the
articles being completed, SPRING offered £100 to £80 that he
won the battle. Monday, December 1, 1823, the backers of the
above 'Big Ones' dined together at the Castle Tavern, Holborn;
but neither SPRING nor *Langan showed* upon the occasion.
However when *time* was called by the President of the Daffy
Club, the BLUNT was ready at the scratch. Some little difference
of opinion took place as to the meaning of the articles: 'THOMAS
WINTER SPRING agrees to fight *John Langan* for three hundred pounds a-side. A fair stand up fight—half minute time to be
allowed between each and every round, in a 24 foot ring. The
fight to take place on 7th January, 1824. Fifty pounds a side are
now deposited in the hands of Mr. H. One hundred and fifty
pounds a-side to be made good at Mr. Belcher's Castle Tavern,
Holborn, on the first Monday in December.' The 'Ould Champion' (Tom Cribb) who attended on the part of his boy, SPRING,
said he had only one hundred pounds to put down; while, on the
behalf of Langan, Belcher insisted that the spirit of the Articles
required £150, and he was ready to put down £150 for Langan.
The dispute in question was fairly discussed by the meeting; and
the President decided in favour of the majority—that if £100
a-side were put down, the articles would be complied with.

On Thursday, January 1st, 1824, the whole of the stakes, of 600
sovereigns were made good over a Sporting Dinner at Tom
Cribb's. When time was called, Belcher showed at the mark on
the part of *Langan* and put down £150. Cribb, also, for his boy
SPRING, instantly fobbed out £150. At the head of the table,
before the President, was placed the Ould Champion's silver cup,
and SPRING's cup was also seen before the Deputy-President.
The dinner was good, the wines were excellent, and the company
separated well pleased with their evening's entertainment.
SPRING was decidedly the favourite at two to one; two and a
half to one was also betted; and in one instance £300 to £100 was
laid. In consequence of *Langan* being a complete stranger to the

Sporting World, the Amateurs, generally, were inclined to bet the odds, instead of taking them.

Wednesday, January 7th, 1824. Often and often as it has fallen to our lot to portray the road and place of fighting, we feel no hesitation in saying, to describe the late scene at Worcester is impossible. It was grand and imposing beyond all former precedent. Upwards of thirty thousand persons were present—nay, several calculators upon the subject have declared, to the best of their belief, that not less than fifty thousand people were assembled together on this milling occasion. It was a union of all ranks, from the *brilliant* of the highest class in the circle of CORINTHIANS, down to the *Dusty Bob* gradation in society; and even a *shade* or two below that. Lots of the UPPER HOUSE; the LOWER house, and the *flash* house. Proprietors of splendid parks and demesnes; inmates from proud and lofty mansions; groups from the most respectable dwellings; thousands from the peaceable cot—and myriads of *coves* from no houses at all; in a word, it was a *conglomeration* of the *Fancy*. Where were you, Mr. Hazlitt? What food for the imagination did it exhibit? Peers, M.P.s, Yokels of every cast, Cockneys and *Sheenies* throwing 'away thier propertish' without a sigh that it costs so much *monish* to witness the Grand Mill. The roads in every direction round Worcester beggared all description. The adventures at the inns would furnish subjects for twenty farces, and the company in general in the city of Worcester of so masquerade a *character* that it defies the pen; and even the celebrated pencil of a George Cruikshank would be at fault to give the richness of its effect. The grand stand was filled to an overflow in every part, with two additional wings or scaffolds erected for the occasion. Ten shillings each were paid for the admission of each person. The masts of the vessels in the river Severn, which flowed close behind, moored on each side of the stand, were overloaded with persons; and even temporary scaffolds about two stories high, out side of the waggons, were filled by anxious spectators, regardless of danger, so great was the public curiosity excited by this event. It was a beautiful sight indeed. Let the reader picture to himself a spacious amphitheatre, encircled by waggons, an outer roped-ring within for the *Padders* and *bluntless* lads, who stood up to their knees in mud. What is termed the P.C. Ring was raised about two feet from the ground, covered over with dry turf; and a cart-load of saw-dust dispersed all over it.—The race-course was so intolerably bad and full of *slush* that all the scavengers and *mud-larks* from the metropolis could not have cleaned it in a week. Outside of the waggons the ground displayed one complete sheet of water; and several lads, who were jolly enough to save a few yards of ground by jumping over ditches, measured their lengths in the water, receiving a complete ducking, to the no small amusement of the country girls, who were putting the *blush* upon the *Cockneys* astray, by their loud laughter—what will not curiosity do? Here the *Swells* were seen sitting down in the mud with as much *sang froid* as if they were lolling on a sofa, tête-à-tête, with some attractive, lovely, fair damsel. Not a place could be obtained in the stand after ten o'clock. The city of Worcester was full of gaiety early in the day; the streets were filled with the arrival of coaches and four, post-chaises, mails, and vehicles of every description, blowing of horns, and the bells ringing, in short it was a perfect jubilee to the inhabitants. SPRING rode through the town in a slap-up set-out and four (Colonel Berkeley's) about twelve o'clock. The postilions were in red, and everything corresponding in *tip-top* style. He arrived on the ground by half-past twelve, amidst the shouts of the spectators, and drove close up to the ropes in a post-chaise. He threw his hat into the ring accompanied by *Tom Cribb* and *Ned Painter*. He was dressed remarkably genteel. At this period all was anxious expectation, and on the *look-out* for *Langan*; *half* an hour gone, and no Paddy; *three quarters* over, and still no Irish Champion in sight. SPRING pulled out his watch, and said, 'It is time'. In the midst of the hour, waiting for the arrival of *Langan*, the right wing belonging to the stand gave way, and fifteen hundred persons, at least, were all thrown one upon another. It was an awful moment. To give any thing like an outline of the feelings displayed by the spectators baffles every attempt—[but] in a few minutes cheerfulness was restored, it being ascertained that nothing material had occurred except a few contusions, and some of the persons limping away from the spot. 'Thank God!', ejaculated SPRING, 'I would not have had it happened while I was fighting, for a hundred thousand pounds!' The *blunt* or stakes would certainly have been claimed by SPRING; but no precise time was specified in the articles; 'it was, as the lawyers say, a *day* in law, meaning any time within the day:' the *time* had not been mentioned in *black* and *white*. Nearly an hour had transpired, when several voices sung out from the stand, '*Josh Hudson! Josh Hudson! Langan* wishes to see you.' The John Bull fighter bolted towards the place like lightning, and, in a few minutes afterwards, shouts rending the air proclaimed the approach of the Irish Champion. He did not, like most of the other boxers, throw his *castor* up in the air, but, in the most modest way possible, *leaned* over the ropes and *laid* it *down*. He immediately went up and shook hands with SPRING. The latter, with great good nature and manliness, said, 'I hope you are well, *Langan*.' 'Very well, my boy; and we'll soon be talking to each other in another way.'—The men now stripped, when Reynolds went up to SPRING, and said, 'I understand you have got a belt on and whalebone in it; if you persist in fighting in such a belt, I shall put one on *Langan*.' SPRING replied (*showing a belt such as are worn by gentlemen when riding*), 'I have always fought in this and shall now'. 'Then', replied *Reynolds* (*putting on a large belt, crossed in various parts with a hard substance*) '*Langan* shall fight in this.' 'No, you won't,' said *Cribb*, 'it is not a fair thing.' 'Never mind,' urged SPRING, 'I'll take it off', which he did immediately. *Josh Hudson* and *Tom Reynolds* were the seconds for Langan, and the *Irish Champion* declared he was ready to go to *work*. The colours were tied to the stakes; and singular to state, *black* for *Langan*, which he took off his neck; and *blue* for SPRING. 'This is new', said Josh; 'but nevertheless, the emblem is correct as to *milling*, (laughing) it is *black and blue*; and I'll take one hundred to one, we shall see such *colours* upon their mugs before it is over.' The time was kept by Lord Deerhurst and a sporting Baronet; and Colonel Berkeley acted as the referee. Two and a half, and three to one on SPRING.

First Round—On stripping, the *bust* of Langan was much admired for its anatomical beauty; his arms also were peculiarly fine and athletic; and his *nob* looked like a fighting one. His legs were thin; his knees very small, and his loins extremely deficient as to strength. It was evident that he had reduced too much in *training*. Langan did not exceed 12 stone four pounds in weight. The Irish Champion was nearly two inches shorter than his opponent. Spring was in fine *condition*; cool and confident, and more than a stone heavier than his adversary. On placing themselves in attitude, the advantages in point of person were decisively manifest on the side of the English Champion, to every unbiased spectator. The combatants kept at a respectable distance from each other; yet both on the look out for an opening. The Champion slowly advanced, and Langan kept retreating backwards, till he was near the stake at the corner of the ring. At this instant the position of Langan was not only fine, but formidable; and Spring did not view it with contempt. The latter let fly right and left and Langan's left *ogle* received a slight touch. Spring got away from a heavy body blow. A pause, an exchange of blows, but no mischief done. . . . Some blows were exchanged rather sharply; when the John Bull Fighter and Tom Reynolds exclaimed, '*first blood!*' 'No,' replied Spring. 'Yes', urged Hudson, 'it is on your lip'. A long pause. Langan made a good stop with his right hand. Some hits passed between the combatants, when they closed, and severe struggle occurred to obtain the throw; both down, but Langan uppermost. This round occupied eight minutes. 'This battle will not be over in half an hour', said a good judge.

How right he was! The battle lasted for two hours and twenty-nine minutes and in one respect it was surprising that it lasted so long as the crowd had invaded the outer ring and for a time it seemed that the fight would have to be stopped.

The inexperienced Langan displayed great strength against the more experienced and skilful Spring but eventually Langan's seconds had to concede defeat when he failed to come to the scratch when time was called for the seventy-eighth round. When he recovered consciousness Langan protested that he could fight on but by that time the celebrations of Spring's backers were in full swing.

CHAPTER TWO

The Social Setting

'Why won't you fight I? I never did aught to offend yer.'
A pugilist, quoted by Capt Barclay

The prizefight has been likened to a Roman gladiatorial combat or a Spanish bullfight, though these were three-handed battles with death as the third protagonist. To the English temperament death was not an essential actor in the ritual drama of courage which the prizefight became. But as in those other dramas of blood the visual appeal was immediate, as was the emotional sensation. The principals in the drama of the prizering made their own plot within the confines of convention and the dénouement remained uncertain. The excitement mounted as the actors demonstrated skill or courage to which few of the spectators could aspire. In no other sport does the spectator so identify himself with the performers and no one remains unmoved when two men fight; but the reaction is not only in the guts, it is in the imagination and it was this dual response that attracted so many creative men as well as the merely callous or insensitive. In their

25

contention the prizefighters reveal a part of what man is like. The accompaniment of brutality and insensitivity is another part of man's nature and was a part of the age.

The common experience of eighteenth-century Europe had been violence. England had escaped the violence of revolution and of war at home, apart from the Jacobite rebellions of 1715 and 1745, but life was lived under a threat of violence, which has to be recognised to understand the character of the people and the sports they evolved.

The nation was at war throughout the formative period of prizefighting, which lasted until around 1813 or 1814, and the sport flourished after the defeat of Napoleon in 1815 until the mid 1820s. (Boxing revived after the two world wars of this century.) It was a time when national survival seemed at stake, and that survival depended on the valour of the nation's manhood. The pugilists were taken as evidence of a valour peculiar to England, as the sport was peculiar to England and certainly not practised by the effete and dandified French. When the Allies, in the persons of the Czar Alexander, the King of Prussia, and General Blücher visited England in 1814 they were treated to a display by the leading fighters as evidence of the toughness and valour of a nation.

One hopes the distinguished visitors were impressed, despite Hazlitt's assertion: 'Foreigners can scarcely understand how we can squeeze pleasure out of this pastime; the luxury of hard blows given or received; the great joy of the ring; nor the perseverance of the combatants'. Certainly it was looked upon as an English art. In the first volume of *Boxiana* Pierce Egan claimed that 'in its proper application [it] has raised the valour and manly intrepidity of the English nation, eminently conspicuous over all others'. Tom Assheton Smith won the respect of the Nottingham electors in 1818 by offering to fight any man who would not give him a hearing.

It seemed quite clear that the bravery of the fighters was of a piece with the bravery of the soldiers and when the two met in the person of Lifeguardsman Shaw even Sir Walter Scott, not a great supporter of the ring, acclaimed him, Thomas Moore saluted him in verse, and Benjamin Robert Haydon carefully recorded in his Diary the details of his death.

But brutality and violence were more strongly in evidence at home than in the faraway Continental fighting. The penal code was based on the deterrence of capital punishment, more than 160 types of felony being punishable by death. There was no regular police force and the intention of the legislators was clearly to control crime by the sanction of the ultimate deterrent. The law was particularly severe on offences against property, and lenient to acts of personal violence. In this the law typifies the age, for violence itself and brutality were not held to be as heinous as the violation of 'order' and property.

In a context such as this prizefighting did not impress its contemporary critics with its brutality and degradation, as it must affect a modern critic informed of the insensitive beatings into which many of the fights degenerated. In an age of very few public spectacles the alternatives to a bare-fisted prizefight might well be an execution, with the condemned man possibly showered with stones, before being hanged to the cheers of the crowd with the hangman's assistant pulling his legs to ensure a clean break of the neck.

Although the Tyburn procession had ceased in 1783, executions were held outside Newgate, and crowds of up to 30,000 would attend. Provincial hangings were equally popular and there were more hanging-holidays than Christian festivals.

It was not until the 1820s that the statutes began to be amended and not until 1837 that capital punishment was reserved for some few crimes only. It should be said that there were many fewer executions than capital convictions, the sentence often being commuted, but there can be safely said to have been more public executions than public prizefights in the period with which this book deals.

There is a curious parallel between the heyday of the prizering and the number of executions, which is of interest in considering the social background of the sport. There were significantly more executions in the years 1813 to 1822 (a total of 980) than at any other period in the century. It was at precisely this time that the number of prizefights suddenly increased (see chapter five). One can press no direct connection between the number of executions and the number of prizefights, nor does the fact that executions were public explain, or excuse, prizefighting, but it is meaningless to criticise the latter in isolation from contemporary events. Gentlemen on the Grand Tour were familiar with even more barbarous public executions and torture practised on the Continent.

In a significant comment William Windham, a minister in both Pitt's and Grenville's cabinets, describes attending a fight between one Hardy and Jack Joseph, 'a soldier who showed upon his back floggings which he had received to a distinguished amount'. The brutality and cruelty of pugilism was by no means exceptional to those to whom such floggings were familiar. This was a time when the press gang operated to man Britain's warships, and when such a reluctant recruit could find himself forced to make his own 'cat' to be flogged for a minor offence. Should he see action, he might have a limb amputated without the benefit of an anaesthetic and he ran the risk of being deafened for life by the noise on the gundecks. This last point is made with great effect by the model of the *Victory*'s gundeck, complete with sound effects, at Portsmouth.

The cult of manliness was actively encouraged in the late eighteenth century, with the very real danger that toughness, brutality and cruelty might be condoned as evidence of manliness. Pugilism certainly was a part of the conception of manliness and its practice was as actively encouraged by the Black Country miners who fought each other for amusement, as the young men who flocked to the rooms of Jackson and other 'teachers'. John Keats' brothers even took a set of boxing gloves with them to Paris. The effete dandies were not typical of the age—they were in reaction against it. The pugilists were admired as much for their courage as for their skill, with Josh Hudson, the Billy Walker of his day, honoured as the 'John Bull Fighter'. 'Game' and 'bottom' were the words used to describe the bravery of the fighter. Wellington's tribute to his mount, Copenhagen, reflects the general esteem in which such qualities were held. 'There may have been many faster horses, no doubt many handsomer, but for bottom and endurance I never saw his fellow.'

Homosexuality was equated with effeminacy. The Prince Regent himself had a strong distaste for homosexuals and this practice was one of the few vices not found among the Prince's circle. To a modern observer, however, the possibility of latent homosexuality must appear in the relationship of some of the patrons and the Fancy with the pugilists. (David Storey's novel *This Sporting Life* (1953) makes this point in connection with Rugby League. There are interesting parallels between modern Rugby League and Regency prizefighting—and it is not entirely fanciful to see Eddie Waring as a latter-day Pierce Egan—a literate, humorous insider taken by outsiders to be the mouthpiece of the sport.) Such questions lead to a comparison of pugilism with such other latent sexual activities as took place in the 'Palaces of Pain'. Punishment as a masochistic satisfaction, both punishment received and punishment observed, was a fact of life, though one usually kept under cover; flagellation was known as 'le vice anglais'.

The fascination which even the most degraded battle exercised upon the minds of onlookers has been memorably described by William Hickey. As I believe that the emotions displayed here were shared by some of those watching prizefights I quote his horrified description. Hickey, as a young man, visited a club called 'Wetherby's' off Drury Lane:

> The whole room was in an uproar, men and women promiscuously mounted upon chairs, tables, and benches, in order to see a sort of general conflict carrying on upon the floor. Two she-devils, for they scarce had a human appearance, were engaged in a scratching

and boxing match, their faces entirely covered with blood, bosoms bare, and the clothes nearly torn from their backs. For several minutes, not a creature interfered between them, or seemed to care a straw what mishap they might do each other, and the contest went on with unabated fury.

We now recognise the sublimation of personal aggression and violence in the catharsis of observed violence, for example in films, in literature and in sport. There can be no doubt that prizefighting provided a sublimation for the aggressive instincts of both the fighters themselves and a good many of the spectators. It seems likely that some at least of the ruling class understood this to be an acceptable safety valve in revolutionary times.

Henry Alken claimed that pugilism had impressed a superior character on the lower orders of Englishmen. Indeed he described a prizefight as 'so excellent a practical system of ethics as no other country can boast, and which has chiefly contributed to form the characteristic humanity of the English nation'. One can only say that humanity was not the principal quality displayed at the average prizefight.

Prizefighting was perhaps a ritualised expression of the pugnacity of the English character. Limited as were the rights of Englishmen in some directions, they could hold pugnaciously to what they firmly believed. There are innumerable examples. Count Pückler-Muskau, a German visiting England in 1826, records that on one occasion he was forced to mount the pavement on his horse. 'This the people regarded as an invasion of their rights . . . a huge gigantic carter held up his fist and challenged me to box with him.' Wisely the count fled.

Dickens depicts Mr Pickwick in equal consternation at the conduct of a cab driver who flung the proffered fare on the pavement and 'requested in figurative terms to be allowed the pleasure of fighting him (Mr Pickwick) for the amount. . . . "Come on!", said the cabman, sparring away like clock-work, "Come on, all four of you." ' Mr Gittings, splendid biographer of Keats, attributes his pugnacity in part to his upbringing in 'the London of Daniel Mendoza, the Jewish boxer, and publican of Whitechapel'.

At school the English characteristic of pugnacity showed itself clearly. Byron is said to have had six fights while at Harrow, and the memoirs of C. J. Apperley ('Nimrod') and George Keppel (Lord Albemarle) testify to the popularity of fighting at Rugby and Westminster. At Eton, where incidentally the boys were said to fight with their hats on, young Arthur Wellesley fought a brother of Sidney Smith, who liked to boast in after years, 'I was the Duke of Wellington's first victory'. Indeed some years after Wellington's departure the boys at Eton were so keen on prize-fighting that a rather priggish young man called James Gaskell says he grew tired of his school fellows, who talked of nothing else but the last fight between Spring and Langan. And it was at Eton that the admirable Dobbin in *Vanity Fair* earned the temporary gratitude of George Osborne by fighting the bully Cuff.

The analogy of prizefighting was used at places of even higher education. Jane Austen's brother James visited his uncle, who was a fellow of Balliol, and removed his gown. He was reproved: 'Young man, you need not strip; we are not going to fight'.

Contemporary opposition to prizefighting was based on a number of reasons, the first and most obvious being that it was against the law, and therefore ought not to take place. *Bell's Life* had an answer to this:

> So do the laws declare actors to be vagabonds, but has not the good sense of modern civilisation slanted and overpowered the legal illiberality. There are numerous laws on our statute books, the strict enforcement of which would do more mischief than good to society and they have accordingly been allowed to grow obsolete by a tacit and judicious neglect.

Mr Justice Burrough, whose prosecution of Jem Burns and Ned Neale for fighting at Moulsey Hurst in December 1824 contributed directly to the end of the old prizering, adduced other arguments. 'We are all aware that these fights are made up for the purpose of indulging the propensities of the vicious and encouraging the betting of the gamblers. Even the men themselves fight for money, and sorry am I to perceive that even those who have some pretence to the rank of gentleman are found to encourage them.' Vincent Dowling in *Bell's Life* admitted there was some truth in this, but he added, little point. Did not all sports, and indeed some other activities, stand accused of the same charge? But professionalism and gambling in themselves were not indictable.

There were other reasons for opposing the sport. Humanitarian ideals were novel at this time and legislation was either enacted, or where it already existed, activated against such abuses as slavery, the exploitation of child labour, and cruelty to animals. It was not until 1835 that an effective law could control such evident infliction of pain to animals as the bull and bear bait and the cockfight, but the battle had been fought for the previous 100 years. Hogarth's prints had aided the reformers in Parliament and William Blake wrote in his 'Auguries of Innocence':

> Each artery from the hunted Hare
> A fibre from the Brain does tear . . .
> The Game Cock clipped and armed for fight
> Does the rising sun affright . . .
> The Winner's Shout, the Loser's Curse,
> Dance before dead England's Hearse.

But perhaps the core of the opposition to the prizefights was that 'the practice is injurious to the orderly habits and virtue of the lower classes' (Justice Burrough again). This solicitude was not humanitarian, but concern for public order. Throughout the whole of the period 1787–1824 there were fears of assemblies of working men. There was always the certainty that where crowds assembled the pickpockets, the prostitutes and the extortioners would be in evidence, and the peregrinations of the Fancy served to disguise the presence of such people in unprotected country areas. *The Times* launched a violent assault on the Fancy and such papers as the *Weekly Dispatch* and *Bell's Life* at the time of

Thurtell's execution in 1824, equating prizefighting and crime.* The *Weekly Dispatch* under its leading article headed 'History and Politics' ran a series of articles, 'The Philosophy of Pugilism', from 4 January 1824, in which it defended the sport and itself from attacks in *The Times* and *The Public Ledger*.

But the greater fear was political. At the time of the French Revolution the possibility of Jacobin rebellion on this side of the Channel was manifest. The Tory Party was consolidated on the struggle against a Jacobin Revolution—law and order is not a new policy for the Tories. It was thought that any large assembly of the lower classes could be perverted by republican, and therefore destructive, action. Certainly the behaviour of large crowds then, as now, was destructive of property. In the Luddite Risings of 1811 to 1815 machinery was smashed, houses pillaged and individuals assaulted.

Radical speakers, like Orator Hunt (incidentally himself a boxer), were addressing crowds, and in the view of the government inciting them to riot; and Hunt's egotistical memoirs picture him as a virile and versatile sportsman in his younger days.

The demand for parliamentary reform was at its height and throughout the country bodies of working men were engaged in mysterious drills, unarmed according to the radical press and armed in the view of the Tory government. The trial of Queen Caroline in 1820 gave further evidence of the violent and destructive potentialities of the mob, with the Italian witnesses attacked at Dover and the windows of government ministers smashed in London.

As the popularity of prizefighting reached its zenith during this period of civil unrest, it was not unreasonable for the govern-

---

* It is interesting to note a remark made by one of the Kray twins to Francis Wyndham and published in the *Sunday Times* of 19 October 1969. 'If you haven't got an education, and if you want to make something of yourself, what else can you do? There's only boxing other than crime, and you can't do that for long.' The Krays were themselves professional boxers before turning to the bigger pickings of crime.

C

ment to fear the vast mobs who attended the prizefights. Indeed, was not the *Weekly Dispatch*, which gave the maximum publicity to the prizering, a radical organ?

In fact, pugilism was not in any sense a political movement, it was an amusement of the people, a safety valve perhaps, whereby violent feeling was directed on a relatively harmless event. The promotions of the upper classes struck a chord in the hearts of the lower classes. The fighters fulfilled the need in the hearts of the people for what we now call 'glamour'. They were the equivalent of today's sports and pop stars; and they came from the working classes. 'Fame after all is a glorious thing though it lasts only for a day,' said Borrow. The bruisers, he said, 'were men of renown amidst hundreds of people with no renown at all, who gaze upon them with timid wonder'.

Prizefighting illustrated some of the paradoxes of the age—imagination and insensitivity, equality and exclusivity, metropolitan and country manners, and glamour and squalor. In an age dedicated to novelty it became one of the fashions of the day.

CHAPTER THREE

The Fighters

A little breath, love, wine, ambition, fame,
fighting, devotion, dust—perhaps a name.

BYRON: *Don Juan*

While prizefighting interested all classes the fighters themselves
came mostly from the lower classes. A study of their background,
occupation and characters throws light upon the social and
economic conditions of the mass of the English people, in a
period of great changes in society through agrarian and industrial
reorganisation.

Despite the attention historians in the present century have
paid to the conditions of the poorer classes, the history of the
later eighteenth century and Regency England is more often seen
through the eyes of the richer and more articulate classes. It was
they who recorded the details of their lives and emotions, and
they who recorded their pastimes and amusements. Dr Dorothy
George has pointed out that much information regarding the
living conditions and actions of the poor must be taken from

newspaper reports on criminal trials etc and such reports emphasise the wickedness or the misfortunes of the poor. So any testimony to the interests and amusements of the poor is of particular interest to the understanding of Regency society. A significant number of pugilists came from the immigrant population, and in particular from the Jews, the Irish, and the negroes. Such immigrants found employment more difficult to obtain than the English, and apart from the Irish they did not receive Poor Law benefits. However, patrons were always to be found for promising fighters, whatever their race, creed or colour. There was discrimination against immigrant groups for a variety of economic, religious and emotional reasons, and in the ring they could achieve a higher degree of social acceptance and economic equality than in any other profession.

There were other immigrant groups in England—the French, the Lascars and the Chinese, for example—who did not produce prizefighters, so one must look for other explanations as to why the Jews, the Irish and the negroes produced, and indeed have continued to produce, a number of fighters. One major reason must be the extrovert or exhibitionist nature of these groups, who have also produced more than a proportionate share of stage entertainers.

In London alone, in 1800 there were between 15,000 and 20,000 Jews and between 5,000 and 6,000 in the provinces. F. George Hay in *The British* says: 'The granting of British citizenship for foreign-born Jews was not made until 1753, and even then the need to take an oath based on the Christian religion resulted in the exclusion of Jews from many posts of responsibility. Full emancipation was not granted until 1858'. No Christian master would employ a Jewish apprentice and this restriction on employment led to a high percentage of Jews engaging in private enterprise, sometimes quite respectably but at other times less so, as the proportion of Jews among the London criminals showed. A number of Jews entered the prize-ring, several of them with great success. Daniel Mendoza was the first to achieve fame as a result of his battles with Richard Humphries. He taught sparring to Jew and Gentile alike and despite his defeat by Jackson in 1795 he remained in the ring for many years, having his last fight in 1820 at the age of 55. Mendoza, despite his well paid victories and his teaching, did not have that gift of increasing his capital which is imputed to the Jewish race, and he was in some financial difficulty when his old antagonist John Jackson refused to allow him the use of the Fives Court for a benefit in 1821.

Another Jew, Sam Elias, or Dutch Sam as he was always known, succeeded Mendoza in the role of the Champion of Jewry in the early years of the nineteenth century. His cognomen has never been satisfactorily explained, though Pierce Egan says he was born of Dutch parents (it might also indicate German origin) and many Jewish immigrants came from Holland; indeed there was a steady movement of Jews between London and Amsterdam. Dutch Sam was thought to be the finest fighter, pound for pound, whom the prizering had known, and he attracted regular backing, which was not confined to his own people. This was significant because the Jewish prizefighters played some part at least in the improvement of conditions for the Jews in England. They had been badly treated in England, the mob often attacking them, and a German traveller, the Pastor Moritz, noted in 1782 that antisemitic prejudice was 'far stronger than it is among us Germans'. The young Jews becoming expert at the art of boxing, however, meant that 'it was no longer safe to insult a Jew unless he was an old man or alone . . .' (George: *London Life, etc*)

Dutch Sam's early death was the result of overindulgence in drink, and he died a pauper, being buried 'without the boards'. Isaac Bitton was his contemporary; while he had none of Sam's genius for fighting, his abstemious character earned him a longer career as both fighter and teacher. Bitton had other qualities, which earned him respect among a wider public. The newspaper *Bell's Life* in April 1825 noted that he was always prepared to appear at the Fives or Tennis Court for the benefit of others.

Bitton was an extremely fat man and his size and character are well summed up in the comedian Jack Emery's rhyme:

> Who'er has seen Bitton behind
> Will ne'er dispute his bottom.

Dutch Sam's son, 'Young Dutch Sam', was a considerable fighter and a contemporary of the Belasco brothers, Aby and Issy, and 'the Star of the East', Barney Aaron. Lesser known Jews who appeared in the prizering included Elisha Crabbe, Ikey Pig, Black Abey, Lazarus, Gidgeon and Bernard Levy, and the strikingly named 'Ugly Baruk' (Moses Levy). Little Gadzee, 'the Catsmeat Man', regularly opened the sparring at the Fives Court with Jem Lennox. The Jews did not escape the censure which they have ever attracted even in the world of pugilism. Borrow claimed that 'it is these that have planted rottenness in the core of pugilism, for they are Jews, and, true to their kind, have only base lucre in view . . .'.

There had been negroes in England since early in the eighteenth century—for the most part slaves freed in England or their descendants—and in 1772 it was estimated that they numbered between 14,000 and 15,000. There was apparently little discrimination on the grounds of colour. Moritz travelled on a coach with a negro and says this occasioned no comment, whereas travelling with a Jew appeared to be resented by the other passengers. But negroes found their employment opportunities restricted. Many remained in domestic employment; the others were likely to be labourers or indeed unemployed. As with the Jews the trades were rarely opened to them in that masters rarely taught black apprentices, perhaps because the negro could neither raise the money to buy an apprenticeship or obtain the benefit of a parish-apprenticeship, though Bill Richmond was one exception. There was a very high figure for negro beggars, in London particularly, where they were called 'St Giles Black Birds', and 700 blacks were offered free passages to Sierra Leone in 1786, a scheme for repatriation with which we find ourselves familiar today. With employment opportunities so limited it is not perhaps surprising to find a number of negroes trying their strength in the prizering, where the potential rewards were far in excess of what they might expect to find in a more regular career.

The first negro to enter the prizering beat Treadaway, a well known fighter in Marylebone Fields on 13 June 1791, but the first to make a reputation was Bill Richmond, who was to have a long and successful career. He was born near New York and came to England as a servant of the Duke of Northumberland. In York he served his apprenticeship as a cabinetmaker, moving to London when he had qualified as a tradesman. After a few turn-ups he entered the prizering in 1804 against Same, who beat him in three rounds. He lost again in his second fight, but then, apart from losing to Cribb, the Champion, he won his next eleven fights and became famed for his science, in particular for hitting and getting away. Richmond became a teacher of the sweet science and introduced Molyneux to the prizering. He was popular with those who knew him and Egan's opinion was that he was 'intellectual, witty and well-informed'. He was a good talker, though he was said to be 'never so deficient as when Molyneux experienced defeat'.

Molyneux was the negro who made the greatest impact on the Fancy. He had come from America to seek the Championship and under Richmond's guidance he was matched with Cribb in 1810. It was widely felt that national honour was at stake and the match created unprecedented interest. Molyneux was unlucky to lose: a combination of bitter cold and malpractice on the part of Cribb's seconds preventing him from claiming the title. In the return fight Molyneux was well beaten and he went downhill fast, dying in 1818. Molyneux's brief challenge had a great impact on the sport and he was followed by a number of negroes anxious to contend for the honours. Kendrick and Sutton enjoyed considerable success and the lesser heroes included the two Robinsons, Stephenson, Jem Johnson, Bristow (Young Massa) and Cropley's Black.

The third group of immigrants to provide a number of prize-fighters was the Irish. Immigration from Ireland had continued from the early seventeenth century and there were large colonies of Irish all over England, particularly in the London boroughs and in the mill towns of Lancashire. The very numbers of Irish meant that there were rarely jobs available for all of them except during harvest time, and, indeed, for different reasons, they suffered from the same discrimination as the Jews. A major fear was that they would take work from English labourers by offering to work for half rates. The younger Irishmen tended to be labourers of one kind or another—builder's labourers, chairmen, porters, coalheavers, milksellers, street-hawkers, agricultural labourers, navigators, and, in Lancashire, weavers—and the older Irishmen were often watchmen; in either case the work was un-skilled and, therefore, ill paid. Apart from the fact that the prize-ring offered a lucrative career, open to anyone, the Irishman has always enjoyed a fight and the game offered particular attractions to the Irish temperament. A visitor to England in 1811 said that the Irish labourers in London 'give each other pitched battles every Saturday night particularly, when heroes and heroines show their prowess at fisticuffs and roll together in the kennel'. George Smeeton in *Doings in London*, 1828, says: 'When the Beadle of St. Andrews, Holborn, was asked if the Irish usually fought at wakes, he replied, "Very commonly" '.

Peter Corcoran had held, and sold, the Championship in the bad days before Johnson and he was followed by Corbally, a sedan chairman, and Michael Ryan, who twice fought Tom Johnson, the two becoming great friends in the process. Andrew Gamble was thrashed by Jem Belcher. Dan Dogherty had a successful career among the lightweights, but perhaps his greatest claim to fame was his involuntary part in ending the ring career of Tom Belcher, Jem's younger brother. Tom hit Dogherty in the teeth so hard that he broke one of his fingers and had to restrict himself afterwards to sparring in the mufflers. Lesser Irishmen like O'Donnell, Paddy Cohen, Fitzgerald, Coady and

Dan McCarthy came and went but the memory of 'Sir' Dan Donnelly remains green for reasons as much outside as within the ring. 'Sir' Dan was said to have been knighted by George IV, and his early death, occasioned by drinking a quantity of cold porter after a game of fives, prompted one of Professor Wilson's *tours de force* in *Blackwood's Magazine*. Wilson, or 'Christopher North', produced a *Luctus on the death of Sir Daniel Donnelly*, which included poems in the style of Byron and Wordsworth, poems in Greek, Latin and Hebrew and a number of other satirical pieces of a rare wit. Other biographers of Dan pointed out his fondness for women and drink, twin dangers that have beset fighters ever since, though not necessarily Irishmen more than fighters of other nationalities.

The Irish also liked to claim the 'Nonpareil', Jack Randall, and Jack Power as their own, both having been born in London of Irish parents.

The fighters of English stock tended to come from the towns rather than the country, mainly because the sport was organised and promoted in the towns. Promising lads would gravitate to a town, and indeed often to London, 'to make their metropolitan reputation'. According to Smeeton in *Doings in London*: 'London is in a pre-eminent degree the metropolis of pugilistic science, the grand centre of amateurs and performers'.

The main source of fighters remained Bristol, at this time the second largest city in England. According to one account, it was remarkable for the orderly behaviour of the lower classes, which nevertheless produced a quite extraordinary number of fine fighters. The Champions alone from Bristol and its environs were Big Ben Brain, Jem Belcher, Henry Pearce, Tom Cribb and Bill Neat. Other Bristolians included Tom Belcher, one of the finest of the lightweights, and Abraham Newton, Elias Spray, Bill Warr, Cyrus Davis, George Nichols, Jack Strong (Cabbage) and that man of bottom, Jack Ford. 'He's a Bristol man' was the highest of compliments to a pugilist, and Lansdown Fair in

Bristol was 'a sort of Nursery, where many of the young novices make their first appearance in the Prize Ring'.

Lancashire, famed for its dirty fighters, produced Bob Gregson and Jack Carter, and Birmingham a string of good fighters, none of whom ever quite reached the heights. There were Jacombs, Isaac Perrins, Stanyard and Fewtrell, one of the first sportsmen to put his name to a book—*Boxing Revived, or the Science of Manual Defence displayed on rational principles.* Later came Arthur Matthewson, Bill Hall and Phil Sampson, immortalised by J. H. Reynolds as the 'Brummagem Youth'.

The only rival to Bristol or Birmingham was London, which produced innumerable fighters dear to the heart of the Fancy— such men as Caleb Baldwin, the Champion of Westminster; Tom 'Paddington' Jones; Tom Owen and his 'boys', Josh and Dav Hudson; Ned Neale; Bill Abbot; and Alic Reid, 'the Chelsea Snob'.

If suitable employment could be obtained elsewhere then the prizering declined, but during times of slump and unemployment, and in post-war periods the number of fighters tended to increase. After World War I almost every professional fighter, including the author's father, was an ex-serviceman, often choosing to fight under their army rank: Bombadier Billy Wells, Sapper Smith, etc.

These tendencies are illustrated in the period from 1790 to 1830. An educational revolution began in England in the early years of the nineteenth century, and by 1830 the number of educated school-leavers showed a significant increase from the beginning of the century. There were jobs to be had for the literate throughout this period, for the wars with France had caused the customary boom in employment, and a number of the new jobs were in the clerical and supervisory grades and demanded literacy. But the number of unskilled jobs did not increase in the same proportion, and, indeed, after 1815 there was a decrease in employment as the country adapted itself to peace. Most prizefighters were illiterate, with little prospect of profitable employment, so after 1815 their numbers increased, due partly to the encouragement of the regular promotions of the Pugilistic Club, but more to the lack of other jobs.

Fighters usually came from the lower-paid trades or professions. In the hierarchy of occupations, the chairmen (sedan-chair carriers) were among the lowest and they were represented in the ring by the Irishman Corbally and by the Prince of Wales' chairman, Tom Tring, a giant of a man who served as an artists' model after his ring career.

Coalmen and milkmen were noted for their roughness and for their physical strength and several pugilists came from their ranks: Ben Brain and Bill Cropley were coalheavers and Bill Davis a milkman. Coalheavers were called 'a very depraved, but useful and frequently ill-used class of men'; around 1800 they took home an average of 15s a week as part of their earnings were paid in drink provided by their employers, who were usually publicans. This exploitation was notorious and it is not surprising that some men saw the prizering as the opportunity to break away into another environment. (One coalheaver, William Huntington, became a noted evangelist [bible-puncher], according to J. T. Smith in *A Book for a Rainy Day*.)

Another occupation which demanded considerable physical strength was that of the navigators, as the canal workmen were known, and it produced a number of famous pugilists. By 1815 about 2,600 miles of canals had been constructed in England in fifty years, and construction continued feverishly until the late 1830s, when the competition of the railways began. The canals were all constructed manually and the number of navvies, or navigators, many of them Irish, was enormous. Colquhoun's estimate was 40,000 individuals employed on canals and in mines. The navigators rarely earned more than 10s per week and their wives' earnings would rarely increase this to more than 15s for a family.

Jack Carter, of Lancashire, who claimed the title when Cribb became inactive, was a navigator, as was Tom Shelton, a violent man but a fine boxer. There were others like Davis 'the Navigator', Weaver, and West-country Dick, who once 'padded the hoof' 20 miles to the scene of one of his fights. Tom Cannon, who beat Josh Hudson for £500, and George Cooper were bargehands on the canals, and Isaac Wood, Lashbrook and Gilbert Parish, watermen, these last being skilled men by virtue of their apprenticeship. Charles Hadfield in *The Canal Age* (p 136) says: 'The natural aggressive tendencies of the boatmen can be seen in the exhortations of "The Canal Boatmen's Magazine" published monthly from 1829 by the "Paddington Society for Promoting Christian Knowledge amongst Boatmen", which begged the boatmen to desist from fighting, as well as drinking and swearing'.

The biggest single group in Colquhoun's population estimate for 1803 comprised artisans and labourers employed in manufactures, handicrafts, buildings and works of every kind. They represented nearly 450,000 out of a working population of about 2 million men and a total population of 9 million, with average family earnings of just over £1 per week, and it was from this group that the majority of pugilists came. Elias Spray and Harry Harmer were coppersmiths' labourers, Bill Cribb and Belton were brickmakers, Bill Wright and Hardy were carpenters, Jack Power was a plumber and Johnson a bricklayer. There was a caulker, Bowen; a rope-spinner, Sharp; a button-maker, Phil Sampson; a basket-maker, Arthur Matthewson; and a mattress-maker, Peace Inglis.

The appalling conditions under which many of the artisan and labouring class worked can be illustrated by the case of the plumbers. For workers in molten lead, the fumes of the lead could lead to paralysis, and Power himself adduced faintness from lead fumes as a cause of his lack of fitness for one of his battles. Plumbers drank quantities of castor oil 'to prevent any serious effects on the constitution from the fumes of white lead'.

Throughout the Napoleonic Wars England maintained a standing army. Her navy was almost invincible, despite the fact that her ships were crewed, more often than not, with men press-ganged in the London taverns or even in their native villages. Jack Scroggins, the most fearless of fighters, was himself press-ganged and served for some years in His Majesty's ships. Other sailors included the Champion himself, Tom Cribb, Harry Jones and John Crockey, who after a brief ring career was transported for highway robbery. And fighters were crimps, or press-gangers, as well! *The Times* in April 1795 reported: 'Mendoza and Bill Warr, finding the blackguard exercise of boxing had fallen into disrepute, took up the gentle art of crimping and became acting sergeants at a house in St. George's Fields'. Serving soldiers were rarely permitted by their commanding officers to engage in prize-fights and Daikin of the Life Guards could only appear at the Fives Court exhibitions. But Lifeguardsman Shaw had two successful fights before leaving with his regiment for Brussels and dying a hero's death at Waterloo. Discharged soldiers like Bone and Joseph were free to fight within the prizering. Jem Berks (Bourke), who was thrice defeated by Jem Belcher, in fact joined the army after a ring career. He became an NCO in a regiment serving under Wellesley in the Peninsular campaign in the Napoleonic Wars.

Other fighters came from a variety of occupations: Hooper was a tinker; Tom Tyne and George Head were tailors, and Head was said to have invented the one-seamed overcoat; and Tom Cribb was an apprenticed bellhanger, though he never completed his time. In the victualling line Nash, Manby, Nosworthy and Jack Martin were bakers, the last known always as 'Master of the Rolls'; and Jack Firby, the 'Young Ruffian', was a waiter or potboy. George Inglesden and Ned Painter were brewers' labourers, and as such could command wages equal to those of journeymen in other less capitalised undertakings.

Land transport, of course, depended on the horse and as many were employed in the ancillary occupations of coachmen, grooms, ostlers, farriers, horse dealers, as are now employed as drivers, garage hands, mechanics, and car dealers. From these occupations came a number of fighters: Bill Wood and Jack Holmes were coachmen, Jack Curtis a groom, Purcell a farrier and Jack King a turnpikeman.

One occupation above all was associated with prizefighting. A number of the greatest champions had been butchers, and butchers were numbered among the most enthusiastic followers of prizefighting and the kindred Fancy sports of bullbaiting and dogfighting. Jem Belcher, perhaps the greatest of champions, had been a butcher and so had those other champions, John Gully, Tom Spring, Bill Neat and Peter Crawley. Other butchers included popular Josh Hudson, the John Bull fighter; Cy Davis; George Nichols; Jack Payne; and Sam Martin of Bath, who fought both Humphries and Mendoza at the time of the revival of boxing around 1790.

The association of butchers with prizefighting is illustrated in *Pickwick Papers*. One of Mr Pickwick's fellow inmates of a cell in the Fleet Prison was a butcher and quite naturally he had been a bruiser in his youth. Mr Roker, the turnkey, described him:

> What a thorough-paced goer he used to be sure-ly! Bless my dear eyes . . . it seems but yesterday that he whopped the coal-heaver down Fox-under-the-Hill, by the wharf there. I think I can see him now, a coming up the Strand between two street-keepers, a little sobered by the bruising, with a patch of vinegar and brown paper over his right eye-lid, and that 'ere lovely little bull-dog, as pinned the little boy arterwards, a following at his heels.

When Neat, the Butcher, was defeated by Tom Spring in 1823 he was heavily backed by his fellow butchers. *Blackwood's* published a mock heroic poem which included the lines:

> But in the shambles of Bristol, among the Butcherly people
> There was blackness of sorrow; loud oaths and sorrowful moaning,
> Ring is the seat of slaughter—but slaughter now was suspended;
> Mute was the marrow-bone now, the ancient music of Britain;
> Cleaver, and bloody axe, steel, hand-saw, chopping-block, hatchet,
> Lay in grim repose; and the hungry people of Bristol
> Could not the following day get a single joint for their dinner.

Blackwood's appended a 'Butcher's Lament', which included the stanzas:

> I was as raw as Butcher's meat,
> I was as green as cabbage,
> When I sported blunt on Billy Neat,
> The ugly-looking savage.

Colquhoun's census records over 500,000 persons as being employed in farming and husbandry, the majority as labourers. The earnings of a family were rarely more than 15s per week, though a cottage and certain basic foodstuffs might be given. Arthur Young estimated the weekly wage in 1770 to be about 7s 4d and in 1811 the average farmworker's wage was 14s 4d, but the price of bread, meat, butter and cheese had more than doubled in this period. Cottages were often let to the farmworker by the farmer.

The system of annual hirings, with the labourer free to move after a year's work, would seem to have allowed a man to change his occupation, perhaps to prizefighting, without much difficulty. Amongst the few pugilists, however, who appear to be from this group were Lenny, a cowman; Tom Oliver, a gardener; and Alexander, a gamekeeper; and it might seem surprising that this large, lowly paid, and usually physically strong group should have produced so few prizefighters. There are a number of explanations. As we have seen, prizefighting was organised as an urban sport and new fighters were usually recruited in towns. A number of country boys became fighters, but they had previously moved to the towns and had followed urban occupations. Among farmworkers there was less unemployment than among urban labourers. Agricultural labourers were in particular demand at certain times of the year and workmen from the towns would move to the country in times of unemployment, which counterbalanced, to some extent, the steady movement from the country to the new urban manufacturing industries. Those farmworkers who remained in agriculture tended to be men with less initiative than their brothers who were prepared to go to the towns in search of higher pay and greater independence in new industries. Prizefighters were usually recruited from groups more ambitious and aggressive than the farmworkers—costermongers, for instance, entrepreneurs ever on the lookout for a way to make money; the donkey dragoons of Westminster produced several fighters including George Maddox and Caleb Baldwin.

Few fighters came from the lower middle classes of shopkeepers or independent tradesmen. John Jackson, whose father was a successful builder, was an exception. The reasons are partly economic, for why should a man exchange the certainty of reasonable earnings for the uncertainty of earnings often only a little higher; and partly social, for the profession of prizefighting was never respectable. There were physical reasons, too. For many men who became fighters the alternative employment was often hard physical toil, and the periodic chance of a hard beating did not appear as a deterrent when weighed against the alternative of grinding work or destitution. But for the lower middle classes the economic, social and physical reasons all combined to make prizefighting a non-starter. Moreover, there were few fighters among those who had successfully completed their apprenticeships, particularly in one of the trades where the apprentice paid a large fee with a view to a partnership, such as brewing, distilling, sugar-refining, soap-boiling, and the making of snuff, colours, printer's ink, etc.

The negro fighter, Bill Richmond, did complete his apprenticeship in York as a cabinetmaker and then came to London to look for work. But in this, as in much else, Richmond was very different from many of his fellow pugilists.

The very variety of occupations from which prizefighters were recruited should not disguise those factors common to men entering the prizering. The recurring facts of background among the pugilists include, aside from youth and strength, an unskilled occupation of the lower classes, an urban environment, the experience of discrimination both social and economic and an individuality and ambition that carried them out of the rut in which

OPPOSITE *John Jackson (F. C. Turner after an oil painting by Ben Marshall)*

they might seem destined to remain by virtue of their birth and surroundings.

Many trades were handed on from father to son, the master employing members of his family as apprentices or workers. This same tendency is illustrated in the trade of fighting, where there were many family connections. The most famous family was perhaps the Belchers. Descended from Jack Slack, who had beaten Broughton, two brothers Jem and Tom were among the most famous of prizefighters and their brother Ned was himself no mean performer. Their sister married Harry Harmer, who remained unbeaten until the loss of an eye caused his retirement from the ring. Other brothers to make their mark were the Balascos, Issy and Aby. Josh and Dav Hudson made a family affair of their fights, travelling together and each seconding or backing the other under the genial supervision of old Tom Owen. Contemporary with the Belascos and the Hudsons were the Curtis brothers, Peter and Dick. Peter died as the result of a fight but Dick remained for some years the 'Pet of the Fancy'.

Sons followed their fathers' profession, the most outstanding example being Young Dutch Sam, who had a worthy career, though he was never as great a fighter as his father. Tom Johnson's son, Ginger Jackling, became a prizefighter, as did Bill, the son of Johnson's great friend and rival Michael Ryan; and Jack, the son of Bill Warr, fought Tom Belcher and won in 1804. Caleb Baldwin was disappointed with the talent of his sons but Bill Richmond's son must have rejoiced his father's heart when he was selected to teach sparring to Prince George of Cambridge.

Cy Davis and Bill Neat were cousins, and Jack Martin, the 'Master of the Rolls', was a nephew of George Head, one of the great teachers of boxing. Ben Burns created great amusement among the Fancy with his loud praise of 'my *nevy*' Jem and Frosty-faced Fogo wrote an amusing piece in *Bell's Life* in which he had Ben extol his nephew:

D

PPOSITE   top left *Bill Richmond*; top right *Dutch Sam*; bottom left *Jack Scroggins*; bottom right *Bill Gibbons* (*from 'Boxiana'*)

> My *Nevy* Jem is broad and square
> Four feet across the shoulders;
> A prodigy they all declare
> A wonder to beholders

The poem ends:

> Huzza! then, for my *Nevy* Jem,
> Huzza! too for his Uncle!
> . . . .
> We are the most surprising pair
> You'll find in all the bevy;
> I, Poet and Philosopher,
> And he his Uncle's *Nevy*.

Bill Neat was content to resume his old occupation as a butcher when his ring career was over. Tom Cannon returned to the Thames barges, Bill Wood to the hackney coaches and George Maddox took his donkey and cart about London buying and selling. But it was not unusual for a retired, or indeed an active fighter to seek some new occupation. According to J. T. Smith in *The Streets of London* (1849) Jack Broughton was for many years a Yeoman of the Guard. 'The Principles of Milling' tells of the customary practice:

> But fighting once over, now each man of war,
> Turns publican quick, and then pleads at the bar

Public houses were important as social centres when there were few alternatives, particularly for the poor. In 1803 there were 50,000 inn-keepers in a population of 9 million. The publicans were sometimes constables, dealers in coal, or promoters of friendly societies or thrift clubs. The public houses were used as paying offices for a variety of workmen as well as the meeting place of clubs and the resort of anyone with the money to spend on gin or porter. Their relative importance was shown after John Jackson had beaten Mendoza in 1795. Jackson, at that time, was a publican, and *The Times* indignantly declared: 'We think it worthy of the notice of the magistracy to consider whether a man who breaks the peace should be a fit person to have a licence as a publican'. Other publican prizefighters at the end of the eighteenth century had similar problems. Tom Johnson took the 'Grapes' in Lincoln's Inn Fields, 'but the customers proving too flash, the licence was taken away'. He also lost the licence of a house in Dublin 'from his house not proving so consonant to the principles of propriety as were wished'.

After 1815 it had become easier to obtain a liquor licence and by 1820 it might seem that the profession of pugilism was a positive recommendation to the magistrates, for a list of fighters keeping houses in that year shows:

Tom Cribb	— Union Arms, Panton St, Haymarket
Tom Belcher	— Castle Tavern, Holborn
Jack Randall	— Hole in the Wall, Chancery Lane, Fleet St
Harry Harmer	— Plough, West Smithfield
Cy Davis	— Bear and Ragged Staff
Tom Shelton	— Black Bull, West Smithfield
Jack Martin	— Griffin
Harry Holt	— Golden Cross, Long Acre
Ben Burns	— Sun, Windmill St
Bill Eales	— Prince of Mecklenburgh Arms, Manchester Sq
Ned Painter	— Anchor, Norwich

This was in 1820 alone. Bob Gregson had held the licence of the Castle Tavern under the name of 'Bob's Chop-House' and Tom Spring succeeded Tom Belcher as licensee of the same establishment. Bill Richmond kept the 'Horse and Dolphin' and old Joe Ward, one of the prizering's most popular characters, kept a house called the 'Green Dragon' where he had a unique gallery of pictures, mostly pertaining to the prizering but including such patriotic prints as the 'Death of Lord Nelson' and 'Duncan's Victory'. Gilby and Cuming in *Life of George Morland* say that Joe had been a crony of George Morland when the artist was dissipating his young genius. The 'Green Dragon' was one of many pubs that sold canaries, which were bred in East Anglia, according to J. T. Smith in *Book for a Rainy Day*. Joe's obituary in *Bell's Life* (3 April 1825) records that 'after he quitted public life, he lived at Paddington where several of his cabinet gems were sold by raffle'.

Whether it was a good idea for an active fighter to turn publican was another matter. 'The landlord must drink with his friends or else be a churl . . . and should he again enter the ring he gives the chance away of two points out of three against himself.' To spell out this warning, there was the danger that 'in serving others plentifully with this luscious liquid he would serve himself so often and so copiously'. Even if drinking did not affect the ring career of a fighter it could affect his reputation. Randall and Tom Hickman became aggressively drunk and drink made Dan Donnelly the more amorous. As for Jack Scroggins, ready to fight anyone at any time, liquor just added fuel to the flames. There were few fighters like Bill Richmond, who could remain abstemious in the midst of plenty. Molyneux, Donnelly, Dutch Sam, Jack Randall and Josh Hudson all owed their early deaths to drink.

In George Head's obituary in *Bell's Life* the cause of his death was made quite specific: 'His predilection for *blue ruin* was the ruin of himself—and scarce three weeks elapsed since he boasted he would drink 16 glasses of gin without disturbing his intellects. That this propensity hastened his final exit, no one can doubt'.

'Fighting men', says Jon Bee, in his *Slang Dictionary* of 1823, 'most commonly take cognomen, or it has been put upon them by the slang-whang reporters, who, when a new man appears, inquire "what name he will go by?" ' The practice of giving fighting men nicknames was long established. A writer in *Bell's Life* pointed out that the usage is as old as Homer: 'he gave every Hero some favourite cognomen, which like a painted label on his shield, distinguished him from all others. The familiar names given to the several members of the prize ring are not less lively or picturesque'. The knights of the early Middle Ages fighting in tournaments also favoured noms-de-guerre. Today's heirs are wrestlers rather than boxers.

Some noms-de-guerre were descriptions of the fighter's trade: 'the Bath Butcher' (Sam Martin), 'George the Brewer' (Inglesden), 'Coachey' (Jack Holmes) and 'Sailor Boy' (Harry Jones). Some described the home area of the fighter: 'West-country Dick' (Richard West) and 'the Brummagem Youth' (Phil Sampson). Others referred to physical characteristics: 'the Black' or 'Snowball' (Molyneux), 'No Neck' (Duggan) and 'White-headed Bob' (Ned Baldwin).

There were titles which were honorific: 'the Champion' (Tom Cribb), 'the Nonpareil' (Jack Randall), and the 'Out-and-outer' (Ned Turner). 'The Phenomenon' was Peace Inglis, 'the Inimitable' George Head, and the accolade of 'the John Bull Fighter' was conferred on the London favourite Josh Hudson. Other Londoners were hailed as 'the Star of the East' (Barney Aaron) and 'the Sage of the East' (Tom Owen).

There were puns. Hen Pearce was the 'Game Chicken', Jack Martin, a baker, was the 'Master of the Rolls', and Tom Cannon the 'Great gun of Windsor'. Tom Spring was born Thomas Winter.

Richard Humphries and John Jackson were always accorded the prefix 'Gentleman' and Dan Donnelly was usually known as 'Sir' Dan, though there is no evidence that George IV did confer a knighthood on the archetypal Irishman. Other nicknames abounded, their meaning more or less obvious. Peter Crawley was 'Young Rumpsteak', Symonds was the 'Old Ruffian', and Jack Firby the 'Young Ruffian'. Jack Strong was 'Jack Cabbage', Charles Grantham the 'Giblet Pie', Jem Lennox 'the Colonel', Dick Curtis 'the Pet of the Fancy' and Jack Atcherlee 'Nacker Jack'. Little Gadzee was known as 'Catsmeat', Jem Ward as the 'Black Diamond' (he was a coal-merchant), and Tom Hickman 'the Gas' or 'the Gasman' (after that substance's incandescent brilliance).

Tom Blake was called 'Tom Tough' after Dibdin's character and Ned Stockman's supporters called him 'the Lively Lad', a most unlikely name to judge from his full-length portrait printed by Fores in the 1820s. One nickname that was well earned was given to a fighter who lost all his four fights: he was called 'Surrender'. There were any number of 'Pets' or 'Chickens' and many extraordinary soubriquets, belonging for the most part to less gifted fighters: 'Hopping Ned' Morgan fought 'Jemmy from Town' at Hennington in 1803, and there were 'Wheeping Mat', the 'Wednesbury Bounce', 'Jack in the Green', 'Gallows Dick', 'Beef à la mode', 'Young Brag', 'Fly-Boy', the 'Yokel Brute', 'Stump Bob', and the 'Chimpanzee'. No Regency novelist need look further than these to give some colourful verisimilitude to his story.

In the age of the dandies there were several fighters who were proud of their appearance, paying attention to their dress both outside and inside the ring. The customary wear in the prizering was a pair of cotton drawers with woollen stockings. Tom Oliver fought in striped silk stockings and Martin, 'Master of the Rolls', on one occasion wore elastic drawers. These apparently let him down as he had to stop and pull them up while Jack Randall was milling him. Tom Owen's boy, Dav Hudson, took a leaf out of his master's book in the matter of style. His arrival at Blindlow Heath for his fight with Ned Neale in 1823 'caused no small sensation among the *Raws* and *Rawesses*. Dav, his backers, seconds, and bottle-holder, all white-toppered, were in a smart drag with four prads of the first going'.

Bill Neat's parentage was respectable 'and a school education followed as a matter of course, superior to that bestowed on the generality of those who turn to the ring'. Neat and his cousin Cyrus Davis were an exception to the illiteracy of the ring, though the prizering did produce a number of 'poets'. It has to be admitted, however, that their work was more noted for the immediacy of its appeal than for any lasting literary quality. The forerunner was Bob Gregson, styled the 'Poet Laureate of the

Prize Ring', who was followed by Tom Owen and George Head, and by Tom Reynolds. The poetry produced in the names of Peter Corcoran, Tom Cribb, Jack Randall and Caleb Baldwin is of a higher quality but is, alas, not by its imputed authors.

It is of course a splendid conceit to suppose that these brutal warriors were masters of the niceties of literary usage, and the correspondence between the fighters that filled the columns of the *Weekly Dispatch* and *Bell's Life* in the 1820s provides immense amusement. The joke went so far as to characterise the styles of composition: 'Harry Holt's for number and unmeaning wit; Tomlinson's in reply for chaff; Neale and Hall's for sham; Peter Crawley's as being the most correct; Neat's for terseness; Tom Owen's for . . .' Jon Bee, alas, explodes all fantasies by telling us: 'very many that appear in type were never sent *to* or *by* the parties but *got up, manufactured, or scribed* for them—some of the alleged writers not even dictating the thoughts printed as theirs'.

Few fighters were sensitive to the arts, but John Langan at least was not entirely 'divested of taste respecting the fine arts'. In his public house 'numerous oil paintings on various subjects attracted the eyes of his customers . . . and music also delighted their ears from the sounds of two first rate piano fortes and songs, sung by professional persons, selected and paid'. Jem Ward became a picture dealer and 'displayed considerable judgement in his purchase of some excellent paintings'.

Although few fighters were literate there were a number not deficient in native wit. John Gully, who earned the title of Champion in 1808, became a coal dealer, then a bookmaker, racehorse owner and a member of parliament. Jack Martin ceased to bake and became a successful bookmaker, and John Jackson continued to amaze the world by his manners and address. But Jack Scroggins, unique character though he was, probably represented the average intelligence of the prizefighter better than say Jackson, Gully or Martin. There is a quite brilliant description of Scroggins in one of Bee's *Fancy Gazettes*, which is worth quoting 'in extenso' as it reveals the personality of that little man and throws light on the general level of intellect of many of his fellow fighters. Before Dickens it is unusual to have such a detailed, verbatim record of the speech of a member of the 'tag-rag and bob-tail'.

Jack is telling his usual story of why he was called Scroggins.

God bless your soul and body, sir, my name is not Scroggins originally; my parents was called Palmer, d'ye see, and we lived down near the Edgware-road, d'ye see, when I was a poor little half starved little thing, no higher than this table here, or that one there. Vittles, and all that, was very dear at that point o' time, you must know; and so d'ye see, as how, I was glad to go any where to get a mouthful of vittles, d'ye see, and I used to draw the beer for the company of navigators that used to resort to the Fox and Goose; that's true, upon my say so,—only ask Mr. Smith, there, that tall genman there, he was my master, and Mrs. Smith, God bless her, she was good to me, very good—'How is she, Mr. Smith, how is my mistress?' Shepherd Smith replies 'Very well, when I left her this morning.' Another voice observed, slily, 'Ah, Jack, you never went to see her in your prosperity, eh?' The little orator hereupon flies into a choking rage of ejaculations, of asseverations, and protestations of his never-ending gratitude, and again appeals to Shepherd Smith as the proof,—he then proceeds—As I was a saying, I was only a dozen years old, with hardly no hair upon my head, and they used to pull it and that there; and I used to resent it upon your great big strapping fellows, till, at last, they used to come across the country for miles, and miles, and miles, and I licked them all one after the other: one Dick Whalley, l——d bless my heart, three times, as big as a church; 'There,' they'd cry, 'there's a little *devil*, why, I'd take and knock his brains out with one hand,' and then they'd take and knock at me over the table, and I used to wait till Mr. Smith gov'd me *the office*, 'Didn't I, sir?' and then I'd let fly at 'em, always licked 'em by dozens. (Here the orator shows *how*; explains by rapidly hitting at the *air*, all the while being a tip-toe.)

There were fighters who were wise enough to invest their earnings and others who spent as fast as they earned. When John Gully became a successful bookmaker he also developed something of the Midas touch: he won £40,000 on two races alone and his own horses were Classic winners. But his patrons had had to pay his debts before he fought the 'Game Chicken'. Bill Richmond was a sensible man and Peter Crawley was praised for spending his money wisely. John Jackson in this, as in all else, remained a model of good sense. Jack Martin had the prudence to marry a wife worth £25,000, though there is a hint in one of Fogo's poems that she was seduced by Young Dutch Sam; and John Langan was able to purchase an estate for £9,000 some twenty years after his retirement from the ring.

One man who understood the value of cash was that splendid Jew, Isaac Bitton. Bitton was having the best of his fight with Paddington Jones in 1801, but

> while sitting on his second's knee, he felt for 1s. 6d. that he had put into his drawers, previous to the battle; not finding it, he refused to continue till he had searched for the same. Mendoza (his second) was quite enraged at this stupid conduct, and urged that the time was expired, but all entreaties were in vain, till Bitton felt the money near one of his knees, when he resumed the fight and proved the conqueror.

It was certainly true that many of the fighters, even those who had earned large sums in the ring, ended their days in poverty. Tom Johnson, who had received over £1,500 for one fight alone, died a pauper, as did Dutch Sam. Bob Gregson, despite four years as a successful publican,

> like many of his class, did not make hay, while it was in his power; when the scene changed, the clouds of misfortune overwhelmed him; and the once sprightly gay Lancashire hero was compelled to take a voyage on board his Majesty's Fleet, not only for the recovery of his health, but to obtain a *certificate* against all future attacks of the enemy.

Caleb Baldwin was reduced to selling oranges in the Fives Court and Jack Firby, the 'Young Ruffian', was described in 1832 as 'so reduced in appearance as to be little better than a mere walking skeleton, almost sans eyes—sans taste—sans *blunt*, and sans everything'.

For the most part, any special skills that the pugilists showed outside the ring tended to be of a physical nature. Charles Grantham (the 'Giblet Pie') was one of several splendid all-round athletes. It was said that he was able to lift seven hundredweight without difficulty, and as a high-jumper, few could beat him. Jack Carter could lay claim to some of the more unusual accomplishments: he was a clog-dancer of considerable talent and 'after the manner of an expert clown, he could stand upon his head and drink off several glasses of ale in that position'. Isaac Bitton, 'a stout, swarthy-looking man with large whiskers and of ferocious appearance', amused his friends with conjuring tricks 'to their intense delight and satisfaction'.

Like prizefighting, the theatre has often had a raffish reputation. Edward Topham was playwright and boxing reporter; the elder Kean was a follower of prizefighting; W. Oxberry, author of *Pancratia*, was a well-known actor; and Jack Emery, the Yorkshire comedian, was a regular at the Castle Tavern and presented the Cup to Tom Cribb. The affinity between the ring and the stage is evidenced in the career of Mat Robinson, who went on sparring tours with Jem Ward and was 'a melodramatic actor above par'. Arthur Matthewson, 'the caresses of whose friends' led to his early death, played the part of Jacko the monkey in a play at the Theatre Royal, Birmingham, and Young Dutch Sam performed imitations of several birds which were 'not only excellent, but truly musical'.

Contemporary opinion of prizefighters was, of course, very varied. Although we shall see the important part played by rich patrons in the promotion of the sport the fighters themselves had no sort of social standing and indeed were generally looked upon as blackguards by the upper and middle classes. The appearance of John Gully in the lower circle at Drury Lane in 1807 caused a flurry of indignation in some newspapers, and the patrician Greville described Gully as one who 'began a system of corruption of trainers, jockeys, and boys, which put the secrets of all Newmarket at his disposal and in a few years made him rich'.

As the Duke of York's racing manager, Greville might have been in a position to know. Perhaps only the lower classes, who have often worshipped sporting heroes as their own champions, really held the prizefighters in any real regard.

The only prizefighter to be buried in Westminster Abbey was Jack Broughton, and it is doubtful if his burial there was in any way connected with his pre-eminence in the prizering. Indeed the dean refused to permit the words 'Champion of England' to be carved on his gravestone. The burial of Hickman, the 'Gasman', gave evidence of another kind of public interest. Hickman died in his prime and his friends, convinced that his body would be 'snatched' for the surgeons, as he was considered to possess a remarkable physique, felt it necessary to bury him eighteen feet deep!

Penny broadsheets, extolling the virtues of real or fictitious boxers, were published by jobbing printers and sold on the streets of London and the larger provincial towns. A typical example printed by E. Hodges of Seven Dials, around 1870, indicates the persistence of the charisma surrounding certain fighters long after the heyday of the prizering. Called the 'Life and Death of Thomas Spring' it includes such stanzas as:

We once had a Champion, his name was Winter Spring
A man both upright and kind,
By high and low esteemed, he was loyal to his Queen,
So brave and so noble was his mind.

Poor Tom Spring was never bought, all his battles well he fought,
In his praise old England would ring,
All classes far and near, so delightfully would cheer,
And their motto was Victory and Spring.

Less sentimental, but showing a rough and affectionate picture of the boxer was a snatch of Charles Dibdin's entitled 'Patrick O'Row', which was sold in sheet form:

Patrick O'Row is my name,
My calling's the trade of a boxer,
I'm a dev'l of a fellow for fame
Why I'm bottom like any game cock, Sir.

Were alive Mr. Slack
On his back
I'd lay him as flat as he's now,
'Tis my washing, my lodging, my food.
Ah! honey, 'twould do your heart good
To be lathered by Patrick O'Row.

In some contemporary attitudes to prizefighters and subsequently it has been as common an error to suppose they were all gay generous fellows as to suppose them all brutes and villains. Borrow claimed that 'prizefighters and pugilists are seldom friends to brutality and oppression'. Indeed we might remember that Isaac Perrins, the Birmingham giant, sang in the church choir and Ben Brain became very religious before his death; that Philip Sampson had been 'intended for a parson' and that Silverthorn, one of the great lightweights, became a Sunday School teacher. And let us not forget the charity shown to the widows of Tom Hickman, of Tom Rowe, and of George Kent and the collections made at the Fives Court for patriotic and humanitarian causes. But there were a number of pugilists whose deeds and actions can find no apologist. Writing in 1823 Jon Bee said that one crime of the London press was that 'it wittingly suppressed . . . the various domestic offences of the rougher boxers'. Bee then instances Tom Hickman (the 'Gasman') who 'brutally broke the back of Davis's dog, and committed the more brutal practice of misbehaving to his wife'. Hickman was generally believed to have caused the death of Old Joe Norton, Master of Ceremonies at the Fives Court. In a fit of temper Hickman had thrashed the old man and Norton died a few days afterwards in Harry Harmer's public house in West Smithfield.

It was, of course, an occupational hazard for pugilists to be provoked to fight while going about their everyday business. What better way for a young man to win his spurs than by beating an established fighter? The gunslingers of the American West suffered the same irritation from this predilection on the part of the tyros. There are descriptions of Tom Cribb, Tom Spring, Josh Hudson and others dealing more or less successfully with this kind of challenge.

Jack Randall had a different excuse when he was tried on a charge of assault against one T. Edwards, a porter, 'whose eye bore sable testimony that he had, indeed, been previously punished'. The 'Nonpareil' agreed that he had beaten Edwards, but claimed that Edwards had refused to pay his bill for lodging and had used offensive language. The magistrate dismissed the charge against Randall and 'the Nonpareil, according to custom, retired victorious'. Randall can perhaps be forgiven for this minor peccadillo as can Tom Cannon for the venial sin of trespassing and shooting game on the premises of others, for which he was convicted in 1825.

The negro John Kendrick, however, was charged before the magistrate with committing a violent assault on the persons of Caleb Baldwin jun, and Thomas Feethy, the driver of a hackney coach in Westminster; John Crockey was convicted of highway robbery and transported for life; while the career of Tom Shelton was marked, like Hickman's, with a violence of a quite unusual kind. Early in his adult life he had tried to commit suicide in surprising fashion. He was drinking with a friend and they began to bet. Shelton soon lost all his money and offered to stake his life. He lost,

and with a composure that would have done honour to a better cause he ascended a lamp-post, tied a Belcher handkerchief round his neck which he affixed, by the command of the winner (his intimate friend) firmly to the post. Pending the suspension however, the handkerchief gave way by the knots getting loose, and the intended victim dropped, no not into ETERNITY, but to the surface of the earth.

Shelton finally ended his own life, at the age of 43, by taking prussic acid in the Ship Hotel, Bishopsgate, but not before he had sold at least one fight and narrowly escaped trial for attempted murder when he tried to strangle Cy Davis with his own neckerchief.

We have said enough to suggest that Borrow's encomiums on the virtues of the British bruiser were overdone. Bernard Shaw, in his preface to *Cashel Byron's Profession*, makes the point that the art of punching should be detached from a general elevation of moral character on the part of the pugilist. Romantic notions of the pugilists should be set aside, for there is no inherent virtue in punching someone on the nose. But when Shaw goes on to say that 'courage is, if anything, rather scarcer, because less needed, in the ring than outside it' he takes his argument too far in an attempt to disabuse the romantics of their beliefs. There were few faint hearts in the prizering and the courage which the bare-knuckle fighters revealed was a worthy quality, whatever its setting. The main reason that the memory of the pugilists has survived is because, in Dr Johnson's words, courage is a quality worthy of respect, even when associated with vice.

It would be wrong to end with a moral or philosophic judgement on the sport and its participants. Seen against the social and economic background from which the fighters came, moral judgements have a peculiar irrelevance. Telling the fighters they ought not to fight would have been like telling the beggars they should not beg. The sport arose from social and economic conditions and any disapprobation of the prizefighters would be better directed at the environment that bred them.

CHAPTER FOUR

The Patrons

I left the place with one wish strongly uppermost, and that
was that I was but a Lord to patronise Jones the Sailor Boy.

John Clare

An advertisement of 1742 reads:

Thomas Hodgkins, from Shropshire
and
Jeremiah MacCarthy, from Ireland
who fought on Wednesday last a severe and bloody battle . . . at
the request of the honourable Gentlemen then present, . . . are to
have a second combat for a great sum of money.

In the next seventy years, until the formation of the Pugilistic
Club, the regular promotion of prizefighting depended on the
financial backing of individual fighters by patrons, who put up
the purse for which the fighters contended, or who backed their
own man against another's nominee and paid their own man,
whether he won or lost.

I shall deal in Chapter Five with the promotion of fights with
which of course the patrons were concerned. In this chapter I
shall discuss the characters and careers of some of the principal
patrons in an attempt to relate the promotion and encouragement
of boxing in this period to the society which provided the
inspiration for the vigorous development of the new sport.

All the leading fighters had their own backer or backers, who raised the side stake and supported the fighter when he was in training. Prizefighting here was in no way different from cricket, where patrons like the Duke of Dorset, Sir Horatio Mann and the Earl of Winchelsea were arranging matches for large stakes, hiring the best available players and indeed often employing them on their estates. Indeed in prizefighting the fighter did not necessarily receive, should he win, the sum staked in his name. He was entitled to receive half the gate money and such money as his patron should choose to give him. If he won, this would tend to be much more than if he lost, and of course his patron would be more likely to back him again. But it was unusual for a fighter to raise his own stake and it was remarked with some surprise when Ben Medley raised his own stake of 200 guineas for his fight with Dutch Sam in 1810.

The patrons ranged from royalty through the various grades of the aristocracy to businessmen, consortia of London Jews and other prizefighters, often publicans. George IV, when Prince of Wales, followed in the footsteps of his great uncle, the Duke of Cumberland ('Butcher' Cumberland of Culloden), who had backed the great Jack Broughton. The Prince backed his chairman Tring, but, like his relative, it is usually suggested he withdrew his support when his man was badly beaten. The Prince was said by Mendoza to have arranged a fight between him and Sam Martin of Bath at Shepperd's Bush in 1787 but the fight did not take place, being prevented by the 10th Regiment of Dragoons, who on the orders of the magistrates smashed up the stage and dispersed the crowd. It would appear that the Prince withdrew from the active support of prizefighting after attending a fight between Tom Tyne and Earl at Brighton in August 1788, when Earl died as a result. The Prince is said to have guaranteed a pension to the widow but never again did he attend a prizefight, or put up any sums of money on behalf of any fighter.

The exact extent of the Prince's participation in the promotion of prizefighting is impossible to assess accurately. The first volume of *Boxiana* says that Tring would have had more fights

OPPOSITE *George Hanger, Lord Coleraine (Richard Dighton)*

LORD

if he had not been 'expressly prohibited', thus suggesting that the Prince could not entirely approve of the participation of one of his staff in an illegal activity. Later ring historians such as Miles and Henning are quite graphic in their descriptions of the Prince's activities, but their sources remain unquoted and their testimony is for the most part of value only where it corroborates earlier contemporary writers.

There is a Gillray print in the British Museum (p 134) showing the Prince, with Colonel Hanger, at the fight between John Jackson and Thomas Fewtrell on 9 June 1788. This was published at the time of the fight and though the evidence of a print cannot be taken as establishing a fact, yet it does indicate that the Prince was at least widely held by many of his contemporaries to be a supporter of the sport. The first volume of *Boxiana*, published, of course, in the Prince's lifetime, records his attendance at the fight between Martin and Humphries at Newmarket on 3 May 1786, and at the fight between Earl and Tyne at Brighton in August 1788. There certainly appears to be no doubt that the Prince attended the fatal fight between Earl and Tyne. And William Windham's *Diary* records the future secretary of state for war hurrying home to write to the *Morning Chronicle* to 'take off, as far as one could, the effect of the accident at Brighton, of the death of a man in a boxing match'. Writing in 1881 Fitzgerald says the Prince was present at this fight and Windham 'was employed to get a palliative account inserted in the papers'.

If indeed the Prince withdrew his support from prizefighting after the death of Earl in August 1788, then his failure to continue to support his own chairman Tring is satisfactorily explained—it was not connected with Tring's defeat by Ben Brain in 1789, by which time we may assume that the Prince had already resolved to dissociate himself from the sport.

But there is no doubt that the Prince of Wales was firmly associated, in the minds of his contemporaries, with support for prizefighting. As we have seen, part of the reason for this association was the Prince's attendance at various fights between

E

above *A prizefight, designed by Henry Alken and etched by I. Clark (from 'National Sports of Great Britain')*; below *Sparring (possibly after George Cruikshank)*

1786 and 1788. Another reason was the continuing and un-disguised interest of the Prince's brothers, the Duke of York and the Duke of Clarence (later William IV), and the Prince's friends —the 7th and 8th Earls of Barrymore, and George Hanger, later the 4th Baron Coleraine of the Irish peerage.

The passion of the Prince and Frederick, Duke of York, for all forms of sport comprehended prizefighting and the original support of the Prince need not be doubted. It is perhaps more surprising to find that the brother who became the most avowed patron of prizefighting was William, Duke of Clarence, for as far as his two elder brothers were concerned he was not considered to be much of a sportsman. Writing to the king in 1783 Frederick described a great hunt, but adds: 'William was not of the party, as he is not a very great admirer of that amusement; besides which, his shoulder hinders him from ever being a good shot, as he cannot bear the least recoil of a gun'. When in America in 1781, the young sailor prince felt it would be beneath his dignity to learn to skate, and instead had a special chair made on which he was pushed over the ice.

Although evidently no active sportsman, William became re-nowned as the patron of prizefighting. His only active participation in the sport had been as a young midshipman when he had had a fight with a marine. His country estate, Bushey Park, was near Moulsey Hurst and his influence in this area almost certainly accounts for the local magistrates long turning a blind eye to the regular prizefights held at Moulsey. Moulsey, or more correctly Moulsworth Meadow, became the main venue for fights between 1804 and 1824 (though Clarence was in Germany 1818–22), and in particular from 1814 to 1824, after which the magistrates effectively prevented further fights in the area. Regular fights also took place at Coombe Wood and Coombe Warren, both within the area of Clarence's influence. That the Duke was prepared to travel for a fight is shown in Creevy's story of how he arrived late for dinner in Brighton, having travelled to see the 'Game Chicken' fight Gully.

Two events in the early years of the nineteenth century showed how royal patronage manifested its interest in pugilism. In April 1814 Napoleon abdicated and retired to Elba, and George, Prince of Wales, now Regent, invited the Allied Sovereigns to visit England at the beginning of June. The Emperor of Austria refused the invitation, but the King of Prussia, with his sons, and Alexander, Czar of all the Russias, accepted, as did the popular General Blücher. The Regent's guests were entertained to an exhibition of British pugilism in the house of Lord Lowther in Pall Mall. Those who demonstrated the native British art were Tom Belcher, Cribb, Richmond, Painter, Oliver and Gentleman John Jackson himself. The guests made suitable comments on the valour and hardihood of their allies. 'The King of Denmark' (1768) is an important painting showing the contrast between typical amusements in different times. The King of Denmark in fact visited England in 1768 and was taken to a foxhunt and cockfight as being typical English amusements.

Many of the same pugilists figured in the other royal occasion, which can only be called bizarre. At his coronation, George IV, the former Prince of Wales and Regent, engaged eighteen of the leading pugilists to guard the external avenues leading to Westminster Hall from unauthorised visitors. The pugilists were dressed as pages and their roster reads like a roll of honour of the prizefighters of the golden age of the ring: Tom Cribb, Tom Spring, Tom Belcher, Jack Carter, Bill Richmond, Ben Burns, Harry Harmer, Harry Lee, Tom Owen, Josh Hudson, Tom Oliver, Harry Holt, Peter Crawley, Dick Curtis, Ben Medley, Purcell, Phil Sampson and Bill Eales. The pugilists combined the role of personal bodyguard with that of 'whippers-out' or 'chuckers-out', the part they were accustomed to play at prizefights when they cleared the ring. Their employment has naturally occasioned debate, for at the time of his coronation George IV was an unpopular figure and the employment of a bodyguard of pugilists seemed the act of a frightened bully. The pugilists, however, seem to have been well able to look after their own public image, for Lord Lennox tells us that 'nothing could exceed the good humour and forebearance that characterised their proceedings'. Their conduct also pleased the new King for 'they each received a letter of thanks from the Lord Great Chamberlain'. The King added a golden coronation medal, which was later raffled and won by Tom Belcher.

As we have seen the Prince's own direct involvement in prizefighting ceased in 1788, but that of his brothers, and also of a number of his intimates, continued for some years. The Prince had surrounded himself with a number of riotous and frequently irresponsible sportsmen including the Barrymore brothers and Major George Hanger. The three Barrymore brothers are often confused, despite the well-known soubriquets by which they are usually known, 'Hellgate', 'Cripplegate' and 'Newgate'. Richard, the 7th Earl Barrymore, 'Hellgate', was the patron of Hooper, the 'Tinman', not only backing him in prizefights but also using him as his 'bully' or personal bodyguard. *The Times*, on 17 September 1791, carried a report on a typical Barrymore escapade. 'It seems his Lordship on his return in his phaeton from the cricket ground where he had dined with the Prince, thought proper to lay his whip over the shoulders of a gent who was driving a one-horse chaise'. The gentleman challenged the Earl to a fight, but when Barrymore appeared to be beaten Hooper stepped in to put an end to the fight. As *Boxiana* put it in 1812: 'His Lordship was fond of *larking*, and whenever he could not come through the piece in style, HOOPER appeared as his bully—whose name overawed, and, many a time, he has saved his patron a good *milling*'.

Barrymore became Hooper's patron in 1789 and the Tinman became a member of Barrymore's extraordinary entourage at his seat at Wargrave in Berkshire, at Brighton and in town. Barrymore backed him in a number of fights, and when Hooper was overmatched against the bigger Ben Brain, Hooper simply kept out of Ben's way until darkness brought an end to the fiasco. 'If I can't win your Lordship's money, I takes care not to lose it', the

Tinman informed his patron. When 'Hellgate' Barrymore died in 1793, Hooper had not lost a fight under his patronage and it was only in later days that he was to lose, and to die a pauper's death. But the fact that Barrymore predeceased Hooper at least clears 'Hellgate' of the charge of abandoning Hooper in his last years. The 7th Earl, who had further disgraced himself by marrying the daughter of a sedan-chairman, died at the age of 24 on 6 March 1793. The manner of his death was as violently inconsequential as much of his life:

> Lord Barrymore, conducting a number of French prisoners from Rye to Dover by the Berks militia under his command, halted at the top of Folkestone Hill. After taking some refreshment, on regaining his seat in the vehicle a fusee which he had carried with him went off and shot him through the head. He died in a few minutes.

In 1792 a journalist Charles Piggott published a scurrilous work called *The Jockey Club* in which he sketched the characters of royalty and the nobility in violently critical terms. When he came to 'Hellgate' even this master of invention and invective seemed overwhelmed. He wrote: 'The eccentricities of this nobleman have rendered him so popular and remarkable that it would be useless to dwell on a character so notorious'. Much the same can perhaps be said of his brother Henry, the 8th Earl, known as 'Cripplegate' because of a club foot. Gronow says that 'Cripplegate' gained his notoriety from 'his love of pugilism and cockfighting', and there is an interesting connection with the world of pugilism which should be mentioned in this context. 'Cripplegate' was famed as the first person to introduce the fashion of 'tigers', namely little boys who used to accompany the drivers of 'Stanhopes' or cabriolets. The first 'tiger' was George Alexander Lee, the son of Harry Lee who owned a tavern by Temple Bar which Cripplegate was accustomed to visit. Harry Lee was a pugilist who fought Mendoza and was a prominent second and sparrer.

A more intimate friend of the Prince of Wales than either of the Barrymores was George Hanger. Hanger was another of those eccentrics who surrounded the Prince in his early twenties. His career was summarised by C. M. Westmacott, a contemporary journalist, as:

> an intimate of the Prince of Wales, an honourable major, who afterwards turned black diamond merchant, who wrote a catch-penny book, with a singular frontispiece to it, with some strange advice in it; and who also published a treatise on rat-catching, and disdained the title of peer which developed to him on his brother's demise.

Some eccentrics are almost predictable in their eccentricities; the Barrymores are in this class, but not George Hanger. His career embraced a series of extraordinary situations. Beginning as an ensign in the first regiment of Foot Guards, he married a gypsy girl, resigned his commission, and went to America with the Hessian Jäger Corps, which had been hired by the British government. He returned to England as a major in Tarleton's Light Dragoons and went on half pay with the brevet rank of colonel. He lived for a year with Richard Tattersall, the horse dealer, and then became equerry to the Prince of Wales and was also engaged in the recruiting service of the Honourable East India Company. About 1797, however, he lost his post with the company and left the Prince's service during an economy drive in the household. Hanger fell into debt and was imprisoned within the rules of the King's Bench for ten months. When he was freed, he set up in business as a coal merchant and his profession caused particular amusement when he succeeded his brother to the title of Lord Coleraine. In 1801 was published *The Life, Adventures and Opinions of Colonel George Hanger*, compiled from his papers in fact by that ubiquitous penman William Combe.*
In 1814 Hanger produced a book called *Colonel George Hanger to all Sportsmen. . . . Above Thirty Years' practice in horses and dogs;*

---

* Chiefly famed as the writer of the first and two subsequent *Tours of Dr Syntax*; also author of innumerable other works, possibly even *Real Life in London*.

how to feed and take care of them . . . the rat-catching secret . . . to breed pheasants. In 1821, at the age of 73, he was known, or at least observed, by the author of *Real Life in London*, living in Regent's Park. He could 'nightly be seen at a public house . . . amusing the company around him with anecdotes of his former days'. He died in 1824.

Hanger's interest in pugilism was undoubted. Charles Piggott described a sparring match between the Major and Tom Black at Newmarket and says that Sam Martin of Bath was Hanger's tutor in the art of self-defence. He was the patron of Watson of Bristol and matched him against Barrymore's Hooper. William Windham tells of attending the fight between Fewtrell and Jackson in 1788, and says: 'the boxing match was in consequence of a purse collected by subscriptions under the direction of H. Aston, G. Hanger etc'. Towards the end of his life it is recorded that, at a milling match, he had his pocket picked of a gold repeater. Hanger was a major in Colonel Tarleton's regiment and Colonel Tarleton was himself a patron of pugilism, appearing as an umpire at the famous fight between Tom Johnson and Isaac Perrins at Banbury in 1788. Tarleton, incidentally, married the actress Mary Robinson, who was the Prince of Wales' first love, Perdita to his Florizel.

It was not, of course, only in royal circles that there were enthusiastic patrons of the sport.

In *Fancyana* published in 1824 Jon Bee listed the principal patrons of the sport over a period of twenty-five years:

1789 Lords Falkland and Barrymore; Colonels Tarleton and Harvey Aston, Major Churchill, Captains Brown and Robinson; Messrs. Hollingsworth, Brown, etc.
1792 Lord Say and Sele, the Lord Chancellor [Thurlow], Hon. Mr. Dashwood, Alderman Macaulay, Captain Halliday, Mr. Bedingfield, etc.
1796 Lord Delaval; Sir John Phillipson; Messrs. Bullock, Clark, Fawcett and Lee.
1800 Lord Camelford; Sir T. Apreece; Colonels Montgomery and Ogle; Captains Desmond, Fletcher and Taylor; Hon.

Berkeley Craven; Messrs. Squire Mountain, Fletcher
Reid, Crook, etc.

1803 Duke of Clarence, Lords Milsington and Eardley, Sir John
Sebright, Captains Mills and Mellish, Mr. Tom Sheridan.

1805 Lords Albemarle, Sefton; Compte Beaujolais; Sirs W. W.
Wyne, T. Shelley, Edm Nagle; General Keppel; Captain
Barclay, Messrs. Brixton, R. Allen, Bangley, Thornhill,
etc.

1807 Duke of York, Marquis of Tweedale; Lords Byron, Craven,
Yarmouth, Somerville, Brook and Barrymore; Sirs H.
Smyth and Clem Brigg; Majors Morgan and Cope;
Messrs. P. Methuen, Harris, Tom Coventry.

1811 Marquesses Queensberry and Worcester, Lords Pomfret
and Fife; Sirs F. Baynton and C. Aston; General Gros-
venor; Colonels Berkeley and Barton; Major Cope;
Messrs. Goddard and Gore.

1814 Sirs W. Maxwell and W. Congreve; Captain Cadogan;
Messrs. Stirling, Graham, Copas, and Rydney.

Bee's list would appear to be in general correct, though direct
participation varied very greatly amongst the names listed.

Many of the patrons were associated with one fighter: Mr
Bradyl—Humphries; Mr Bullock—Tom Johnson; Mr Elliot—
Tom Hickman; Sir Thomas Apreece—Mendoza; Captain Robin-
son—William Wood; Major Morgan—Bob Gregson; Colonel
Barton—Jack Randall; Mr Ephraim Jacobs—Dutch Sam; and
Mr Hayne—Tom Cannon.

Amongst the more active patrons were Alderman Harvey
Christian Coombe, Colonel Harvey Aston, Mr Fletcher Reid and
Captain Barclay. Coombe's name is several times recorded as an
umpire at prizefights, including the second battle between Humphries and Mendoza in 1789, when he appeared as Humphries'
umpire. Coombe was both an alderman and was four times
returned as MP for the City of London.

Harvey Aston, a dandy who bought twenty shirts at a time, is
said to have introduced John Jackson to the prizering, and he
also acted as umpire in a number of prizefights. Colonel Aston's
death in India was reported in *The World* in 1799. The circum-

stances were unusual. He had been absent from his regiment for a short time and when he returned he had reason to criticise two majors. The majors took the matter personally and the Colonel had to fight two duels. In the first his opponent's pistol snapped, which was declared equal to a fire by the seconds; Colonel Aston fired into the air, saying he had no quarrel with his major. In the second duel the major concerned fired first, but Colonel Aston appeared unhurt and levelled his gun with a steady hand to show he was able to fire. He then drew the pistol back saying: 'I am shot through the body; I believe the wound is mortal, and therefore decline returning the fire, for it never shall be said that the last act of my life was dictated by a spirit of revenge'. He was carried home, where he languished in agony for several days, and without a murmur expired. It was Aston's death, incidentally, which gave young Arthur Wellesley (later Duke of Wellington) the opportunity of an enlarged command in his first great campaign in Mysore.

Mr Fletcher Reid was perhaps the most active of all patrons, for he backed Jem Belcher, Tom Belcher, John Gully, Bill Ryan (Michael's son), and Bill Richmond at various times. He was a native of Dundee and succeeded to his mother's estates only two days before his own death on 24 January 1807.

Miles records that the following lines, in rather questionable taste, appeared in a monthly publication, after his sudden demise:

> In the still of the night, Death to Shepperton went,
> And there catching poor Fletcher asleep,
> He into his wind such a finisher sent
> That no longer 'the time' could he keep.

He has also been described as one of those invaluable persons who deem losing the next greatest pleasure to winning, and who would rather back the weaker side than no side at all.

The most celebrated of all patrons, however, was Robert Barclay Allardice, commonly known as Captain Barclay. He backed John Gully and Tom Cribb, and he was himself an

enthusiastic sparrer. Barclay's fame springs chiefly from his own
athletic achievements, in particular as a pedestrian, and from the
training regimen which he recommended for both pedestrians
and boxers. He inherited immense physical strength and at the
age of 20 he lifted a man of eighteen stone from floor to table
level with one hand. He won a number of wagers for his prowess
as a pedestrian: his most extraordinary achievement was to walk
1,000 miles in 1,000 hours, walking one mile in each successive
hour. The wager created enormous interest and his progress was
followed day by day in the papers (see *The Globe*) with reports on
his physical condition.

He claimed the earldom of Airth, on the grounds of his descent
from William, Earl of Monteith (d 1694). The case was heard
before the House of Lords in 1839, and in 1840 he claimed also
the earldoms of Strathern and Monteith, but proceedings were
dropped. In 1842 he published an account of an agricultural tour
of the United States and he died in 1854 at the age of 75 as a
result of a kick on the head from a horse.

With the formation of the Pugilistic Club in 1814 the private
patron was less in evidence, though by no means extinct, as
witness the activities of Mr Elliot, Tom Hickman's backer and
Mr Hayne (Tom Cannon). The Pugilistic Club was formed by a
number of patrons of prizefighting. 'It had a regular secretary and
treasurer, and consisted of about 120 subscribers, at a certain sum
annually from which fund purses were given according to the
various degrees of the boxers. The highest subscription purse was
fifty and the lowest ten guineas.' The most emphatic article of the
Club was 'the expressed determination of the members to expose
all *crosses* (ie, boxers selling their battles) and to prevent those
persons in any transactions of this kind'.

The Club had its own ring stakes, on which were painted the
letters PC, and ropes which were used for all the fights it arranged.
The stakes were kept by Bill Gibbons, who was appointed the
official ringmaker.

The stakes and ropes were used for the first time on 3 May

1814 at Coombe Wood when Bill Richmond met Davis the 'Navigator' for the first purse presented by the Club, one of £50.

The members of the Club were dressed in their uniform (blue and buff, with yellow kerseymore waistcoats, with P.C. engraved on their buttons); and those persons appointed to clear out the outer ring wore dark blue ribbons in their hats to designate their appointment, tending to prevent any sort of confusion, which at other times men so acting have been challenged with officiousness.

The Club held its first public dinner on 22 May 1814, with Sir Henry Smith, Bt, in the chair and Lord Yarmouth as the principal speaker.

The idea of the Club had been canvassed at Jackson's rooms and its formation was a natural development in the administrative organisation of a sport liable to the corruption or the deliberate misunderstanding of rules consequent on its association with gambling. Racing had the Jockey Club, the stewards of which were the arbiters of the sport, and cricket had the MCC, which had steadily become recognised as the fountainhead of declared wisdom with regard to the rules and the organisation of the sport. Indeed the Pugilistic Club proved disappointing in so far as it was a short-lived institution compared to the eternal headquarters of cricket and racing. But for a time it was the most important patron of prizefighting. Contemporary opinion was that:

> The high respectability which they confer by the patronage of their rank is of inestimable benefit . . . also by the substantial rewards to valour which their united funds enable them to bestow. Much difficulty had often been experienced in raising a purse to be contended for in battle. Many displays of heroism were thus prevented. But as every member of the Club contributed his subscription, there are always funds ready, which the voice of the society may devote to the proper purpose.

I have left until last the most outstanding man of all those who patronised the sport, whether with their cash or by their presence at fights. The most distinguished patron, judged by his character and abilities, was undoubtedly William Windham, one of the outstanding men in an age of all the talents. The tributes to him in contemporary memoirs, when assembled, are almost too glowing in their praises. To Macaulay, Windham was 'The first gentleman of his age, the ingenious, the chivalrous, the high souled Windham'. To Fanny Burney he was 'one of the most agreeable, spirited, well-bred and brilliant conversers I have ever spoken with'. Sir Nathaniel Wraxall declared that 'over his whole figure, nature had thrown an air of mind . . . his conversation displayed the treasures of a highly cultivated understanding'. The highest rank he reached in public life was Secretary for War and Colonies in Grenville's Ministry of all the Talents. He died in 1810.

Windham was educated at Eton, and was said to have been 'a sound cricketer, a skilful oarsman, and so useful too, with his fists that he was known as "Fighting Windham" '. But the boy was a considerable classical scholar and retained throughout his life the attitudes and manners of the intellectual. He was recognised as one of the finest of speakers in a parliamentary age which valued oratory as an art.

In 1780 he suffered an illness which had a profound effect on his attitude to life. The fear of being cut short before fulfilling his public ambitions made him endeavour to waste not a moment of life in inaction; indeed he felt he must exercise his talents to the full. This determination had at least one side effect which we must regret, for his diary remained for the most part a simple register of names of people he had met, rather than detailed descriptions of the meetings. His circle included the most distinguished and brilliant men and women of the day and his brevity is the more to be regretted. His diary for some few days in May 1789, for example, reads:

	25th	Dinner at Sir Horace Mann's
	26th	Boodle's Ball
	27th	Westminster Hall
June 1st		Dinner at Douglas's. Went with Sneyt to Lord North's.

What would a Gronow, or a Creevy, have done with such material? But the point to be made is that it is extraordinary that with his character and ability, and his avowed determination to avoid the less important things in life, he should not only have attended so many prizefights, but should have written about them in such detail, when compared to his usual frugal diary entries. His enthusiasm for prizefighting became legendary in his own time. Tom Moore wrote in 1811: 'I suppose you have heard that during the "Talents" administration Windham received an express from Lord Grey, which made a sensation in every town it passed through, but which turned out to be the "announce" of a battle between Gully and Gregson, sent by the Foreign Secretary to the War Secretary'.

When Windham made a balloon ascent in May 1785, his great friend Burke wrote to him: 'I think you are the first rational being who has ever taken flight'. If one substitutes 'fight' for 'flight' it would still be a fair comment, for Windham's industry in attending and justifying prizefights was striking. He records in his diary attending over twenty prizefights, including such famous battles as Humphries v Martin, Mendoza v Martin, Johnson v Ryan, Fewtrell v Jackson, Cribb v Nichols, and Gregson v Cribb. He records his regret at missing a debate in the House of Commons to attend the battle between Johnson and Ryan; he also regrets letting himself 'be drawn by Boswell to explore . . . Wapping, instead of going when everything was prepared, to see the battle between Warr and Stanyard, which turned out a very good one, and which would have served as a very good introduction to Boswell'. He records the day of the battle between Gully and Gregson after an entry in which he offers a textual amendment to the funeral oration by Pericles as printed in the Bipart edition of Thucydides.

Windham remained a tireless supporter of the 'Old English Sports'; the bill to abolish bearbaiting was rejected by the Commons in 1802 chiefly due to his vigorous opposition. As a defender, indeed as a proselytiser of pugilism, he was unequalled.

It was he who gave John Jackson the famous print of a Roman scene in which an assassin flees, dagger in hand, leaving women and children shrieking in agony over the body of his victim. The inscription read:

FROM THE RIGHT HON W. WINDHAM, M.P. TO MR. JACKSON

Humbly recommended to the consideration of those who are labouring to abolish what is called the brutal and ferocious practice of boxing.

Let us leave the patrons of prizefighting with a justification of the sport, penned by the most coherent of their number in a letter to a Mr Hudson of Warwick in 1809:

A smart contest this between Maddox and Richmond! Why are we to boast so much of the native valour of our troops at Talavera, at Vimeiro, and at Marida, yet to discourage all the practices and habits which keep alive the same sentiments and feelings? The sentiments that filled the minds of the 3,000 people who attended the two pugilists were just the same in kind as those which inspired the higher combatants on the occasions before enumerated. It is the circumstances only in which they are displayed, that makes the difference.

'He that the world subdued, had been
But the best wrestler on the green.'

There is no sense in the answer always made to this, 'Are no men brave but boxers?' Bravery is found in all habits, classes, circumstances and conditions. But have habits and institutions of one sort no tendency to form it, more than of another. Longevity is found in persons of habits the most opposite, but are not certain habits more favourable to it than to others? The courage does not arise from mere boxing, from the mere beating or being beat; but from the sentiments excited by the contemplation and cultivation of such practices. Will it make no difference in the mass of a people, whether their amusements are all of a pacific, pleasurable, and effeminate nature, or whether they are of a sort which calls forth a continued admiration of prowess and hardihood? But when I get on these topics, I never know how to stop.

CHAPTER FIVE

Development and Promotion

Then to the crowded circus forth they fare:
Young, old, high, low, at once the same diversion share.
The lists are oped, the spacious area cleared,
Thousands on thousands piled are seated round.

BYRON: *Childe Harold's Pilgrimage*

Prizefighting did not develop in isolation; no major sport can do so, and pugilism was very much the child of an age. It was not, of course, the only major spectator sport in the period, and so we shall look first at those other sports which developed at the same time. In the period 1780–1824 they were racing, cricket, cockfighting (often organised as a double bill with racing), dogfighting, and bullbaiting. Hunting, fishing and coursing, popular participant sports, attracted no spectators and so are outside the present consideration.

Racing was the most organised of all sports, with a massive capital investment in terms of bloodstock and of land, where the major racecourses, Newmarket, Epsom, Ascot, Doncaster and Goodwood, were already established with splendid grandstands and other spectator facilities. Indeed there were a great number of country racecourses at which annual or biannual meetings were held. The Jockey Club was founded in 1752 and in a short period had taken over the organisation of a sport which had been popular but unorganised for over 100 years. The Pugilistic Club, founded in 1814, was clearly based on the Jockey Club, with the fixtures, prizes, and rules laid down by a respectable body to whom appeals on disputes could be made. Before the establishment of the Jockey Club there had been few detailed codes of conduct with regard to riding, and jostling and cramming had been regular features of the races. Its influence undoubtedly helped racing develop by making it more respectable and helping to cut out the worst malpractices, so that a bet could be laid on the basis of known hazards. The Pugilistic Club, though never as powerful as the Jockey Club, conferred similar benefits on the sport of prizefighting.

The Jockey Club established the five classic races between 1776 and 1814, thus reorganising the whole sport of racing. The Pugilistic Club did much to reorganise prizefighting by establishing venues—Moulsey Hurst, Coombe Wood, Coombe Warren, with a London headquarters at St Martin's Lane. And the PC also helped standardise the ring size and type, and its influence on codes of conduct was to be ratified in the 1838 Rules. The members of the Jockey Club and the Pugilistic Club were all from the top 'Ten Thousand' from which the country's rulers came. At this time only such a group could influence the organisation of a sport on a national scale.

Money for the promotion of racing was provided only from the racehorse owners. Enclosed meetings and gate money were unknown and, as with boxing, the stake had to be provided independent of the gate. In the second half of the eighteenth century there were in fact a large number of 'matches', one horse against another, with the owners putting up a side stake of anything between £50 to £2,000. Another common practice was the 'sweepstake' race in which the owners put in money to provide the prizes.

Three of the charges often laid at the door of prizefighting—cruelty, corruption and unruly crowd behaviour—can be directed with equal justice at racing. In the eighteenth century the distances of many races were much more punishing than nowadays and the system whereby animals are forced to run to the limit, under the whip and spur, while carrying artificial weights was certainly cruel, as many contemporary racing men were quick to point out. As for corruption, the doping of horses and the malpractice of jockeys were not unknown; Daniel Dawson, for example, was executed for poisoning a horse in 1812 and Sam Chiffney Senior was warned off Newmarket Heath in 1791 after the Stewards of the Jockey Club were satisfied that he had not ridden to win on the Prince of Wales' horse 'Escape'.

As for crowd disorder, it was as familiar a problem at race meetings as at prizefights. The experiences of the artist George Morland were not unique. Morland was himself a jockey and at Mount Pleasant, near Margate, when he failed to win on the favourite, he was surrounded by an angry mob who used their whips on him. At Margate races when he rode a winner, he was attacked by '400 sailors, smugglers, fishermen, etc., with sticks, staves and fists'. He was pulled to the ground, and saved from a mortal beating only by the intervention of a party of horsemen. Indeed even the *Sporting Magazine* was to declare, in 1806:

From the number of accidents that have happened by the interference of drivers and the crowds on the course at Epsom, it has been agreed that there shall not be any races run after dinner, and it is imagined that the Derby and Oaks will shortly be transferred to some other place.

F

The Act of 1740, pertaining to racing, anticipated that of 1750, directed against pugilism. The former act sought

> to remove all temptation from the lower class of people who constantly attend the races to the great loss of time and hindrance of labour, and whose behaviour still calls for stricter regulation to curb their licentiousness and correct their manners.

There are a number of parallels between the organisation of cricket and that of prizefighting and racing. Cricket had been played for centuries in an elementary form but it was not until the second half of the eighteenth century that it became organised and attracted large numbers of spectators. As with prizefights, cricket was organised in the first instance by patrons who put up a side stake for their own team. Patrons like Lord Winchelsea, the Duke of Dorset, the Earl of Tankerville and Sir Horace Mann, retained cricketers on their staffs as estate servants, etc, in a similar fashion to the patronage of the prizefighters (cf Lord Barrymore and Hooper, the 'Tinman'). 'Silver Billy' Beldham once described the situation to the Rev James Pycroft: 'The match seemed like Sir Horace Mann and Lord Winchelsea and their respective tenants—for when will the feudal system be quite extinct'.

The Marylebone Cricket Club was formed in 1787 and came, like the Jockey Club and to a lesser extent the Pugilistic Club, to control the organisation of the fixtures, the venues, and the rules and conduct of its sport. It likewise raised sums from its members for prize money, thus taking over the role of the private patrons in the promotion of the sport. As with pugilism and racing, large crowds were attracted to the better organised and widely advertised games, but gate money, though sometimes charged, was not the basic prize.

There were, in cricket, as in prizefighting and racing, the problems of corruption and crowd control. The bookmakers were strongly in evidence at Lord's until 1825, when the MCC banned them. Mary Russell Mitford, herself a cricket enthusiast, described them in 1823:

There they stood, railed in by themselves, silent, solemn, slow, playing for money; making a business of the thing—people who make a trade of that noble sport, and degrade it into an affair of betting and hedging and cheatings.

One of the greatest of the professionals, William Lambert, was forced to leave cricket when sufficient evidence was produced that he had thrown away a game; there were even suggestions that Sir Frederick Beauclerk himself was not entirely guiltless of sharp practice.

Large crowds watched the big matches—20,000 were said to have watched Kent play Hampshire in 1772 at Sir Horace Mann's ground at Canterbury, and the popularity of the sport increased after that date. When Pitt, in 1803, introduced an amendment to the Defence Act concerning the mobilisation of the local militia he specified a limitation of six miles distance between a man's house and the place of assembly: 'The distance ... is not more than the sturdy English peasantry are in the habit of going when led to a cricket match'. The crowds were frequently riotous—the fact that newspaper reports occasionally state that the spectators behaved well being rather an indictment of their more usual behaviour. In 1787 when Leicester had beaten Coventry there was a pitched battle in the streets of Hinckley.

There were many incidental similarities between cricket and prizefighting. There were patrons who promoted both sports, men like the Duke of Hamilton, Sir Charles Lennox, later 3rd Duke of Richmond, the 7th Earl of Barrymore and others. Articles of Agreement were drawn up and published for the big games, and the colours of the combatants were sported by the supporters. There were public houses favoured by the Fancy—in London the most renowned amongst cricketers was 'The Green Man and Still'. 'There was no mistaking the Kent boys', said Billy Beldham, 'when they came staring into the Green Man. A few of us had grown used to London, but Kent or Hampshire men had but to speak, or even show themselves, and you need not ask them which side they were on.' From time to time, as in

prizefighting, special arrangements would be made for spectators
—the Duke of Portland planned a ground to include 'the effect
to the spectators, and the superior convenience of refreshments',
and George Osbaldeston, a keen cricketer amongst his other
sporting interests, had two huge marquees erected when he
organised a match near York. Both cricket and prizefighting
encouraged the advent of large numbers of professional sportsmen, and both sports, incidentally, were honoured with master-
pieces of description by William Hazlitt.

A last word on the sports contemporary with prizefighting
concerns cockfighting and the sports of the people—dogfighting
and bullbaiting. Cockfighting could claim considerable antiquity
and remained immensely popular throughout the eighteenth
century and indeed until it was restricted by statute in 1835.

The cockfight clearly has a resemblance to the prizefight.
Alken, who was less sensitive to pain inflicted on cocks than on
horses, described a cockfight as 'a legitimate object of curiosity,
in which we admire, in their voluntary combats, the fierce
courage, steady resolution, activity and native skill of these . . .
animals'. The same description could be applied to a prizefight.
But there was more than a superficial similarity between prizefighting and cockfighting. As with pugilism there was the unorganised cockfight, the shagbag, or shakebag fight, in which the
cock was shaken out of his bag to do battle for a small wager. This
was akin to the 'turn-up' in pugilism. But the main cockfights
were very much organised affairs, with Articles of Agreement,
almost exactly similar to those of the prizering, being drawn up
stating the amount of the stake, the principals, the venue, the
rules, etc.

There were great patrons who retained feeders, and who had
literally hundreds of birds, staking large sums of money on
'mains' of cocks, often organised in the mornings and evenings of
race-meetings. The 12th Earl of Derby was the most famous of
these patrons, retaining the equally celebrated Joseph Gilliver as
his 'feeder' or 'trainer'. In the pit itself the 'feeder' would hand

over the bird to the 'setter-to', the parallel to the second in the prizering.

But the real similarity between cockfighting and pugilism was also shared with those other 'sports', dogfighting and bullbaiting. This was the crowd, which attended all these so called 'Fancy Sports'. The brutality attracted people of a like mind, and, as I shall indicate later, they represented a large number of the population. 'Cruelty' and 'brutality' are terms depending more on emotional than objective criteria, but insensitivity is a charge more easily sustained.

Crabbe's lines on the cock fancier applies equally to the majority of the Fancy:

> He damns the craven fowl that lost his stake,
> And only bled and perished for his sake.

Prizefighting was then not unique in its development and organisation. There were similar patterns in the progress of the other major contemporary spectator sports, not least for the reason that the organisers were patrons of several sports. But before we look at the promotion of pugilism, we must ask the more general question as to why a number of sports were re-organised in the second half of the eighteenth century. Why was it at this time that rules were published, that a new group of professional sportsmen appeared bringing enormous improvements in technique and practice, and that sports which had existed locally made an impact nationally?

All the sports we have discussed were promoted primarily for the purpose of gambling by the promoters. They were not promoted as spectator sports, for extrance money was not always charged and it was certainly not an integral part of the promotion. Indeed, as we shall see, a large crowd was a frequent embarrassment to the promoters, on occasions causing cancellations of events. The spectators then were not encouraged to come, but they came in large numbers because of the inherent attraction of these old sports, made more attractive by the large wagers which were known to depend on their result. The larger the wager, the more attractive to spectators, as the participants were likely to reveal more courage and skill.

But the promotion of the sports was founded on the stake money the promoters were prepared to put down, and it was the side stake which dictated that clear-cut rules should be drawn up and that impartial arbiters should ensure that the rules were adhered to. The arbiters were the umpires, referees and judges and the rules were declared both generally and specifically in Articles of Agreement. These articles were common to prize-fighting, cricket, cockfighting and even racing, where articles were drawn up for many of the matches made.

The interest and excitement of one wager generated another, and as it was the successful protagonists who were, naturally, in more demand, the quality of the sports increased with the quantity. The promoters' stakes were only the first of many, as the spectators also backed their fancy with their fellows or with the blacklegs, or bookmakers, who were available at the scene of the sport or at such meeting places as Tattersall's and Lord's.

The sports would not have developed in this organised fashion had not the passion for gambling been widespread. Gambling was a stimulus enjoyed by 'old, young, hale and infirm', and indeed one can add male and female. Gambling and drinking were perhaps the two most popular pastimes of the urban worker and he could indulge in both at the public house where he was often paid his wages. Best of all was to bet on your fancy, and the horse, the dog, and the pugilist attracted the greatest number of backers. Among the upper classes the greatest amounts of money were lost on the turf and at the card table but the prizering provided an entertaining alternative for many.

The improvement in communications helped in the development of sport as a national rather than a local pastime. Apart from the despatch of homing pigeons after the fight and the crowds waiting at toll gates down the route, results and often reports began to be carried in the newspapers and the result of a fight at

Moulsey could be known in Birmingham almost as soon as London. 'Pierce Egan's Courier may be had by Post, on Sunday, Two Hundred Miles from London' was the proud boast of the editor.

The fact that prizefighting was declared to be illegal by an act of parliament in 1750 caused a number of problems in the promotion and organisation of fights. The venue could rarely be advertised well in advance of a fight and so tickets could not be sold in advance. As the number of spectators and the amount of gate money remained unpredictable, it was necessary for the prize money to be guaranteed beforehand, usually by a private patron, or a group such as the members of the Pugilistic Club. Any money taken at the gate was usually divided equally between the two fighters.

There was one promotion in 1824, for the second fight between Spring and Langan, in which an entrepreneur acted like a modern promoter by guaranteeing the fighters' prize money in advance and organising the venue to recoup his expenses from the gate money.

The entrepreneur, or promoter, in question was one Mr Hewlings, of the Swan Inn, Chichester. Confident that the magistrates would not interrupt the fight Hewlings undertook to guarantee the fighters £200 and he hired a field and erected a wooden stage at his own expense. 'The field was bordered by the canal and it was only approachable by means of a draw bridge over which all must necessarily pass to the ring side, and at which a toll was imposed on all comers.' This promotion is of particular interest because it contains a number of unusual features. Firstly it is surprising that a sum of money was guaranteed to both fighters by a third party.

In Broughton's days when the fights were freely advertised in the press a typical advertisement read:

> At the Great Booth at Tottenham-Court, this Day, being the 11th instant, will be a smart Trial of Manhood between the 2 following champions

I, James Gladman, Carman, from Puddle-Dock, who am well known for my Manhood and Bravery, who made so long and terrible a Battle with John Davis the Chairman, do invite that proud Hibernian Patrick Henley to fight me at the Time and Place above-mentioned, for the sum of Five Pounds, not doubting but that I shall serve him as I have all others that I ever enjoyed, and hope to give entire Satisfaction to all Gentlemen that will honour me with their Company.

James Gladman

I, Patrick Henley, will not fail meeting this bold Challenge at the Place appointed, and fight him on his own terms, and don't doubt but I shall make him repent his rash Attempt, which shall be the earnest Endeavour of me,

Patrick Henley

The Doors will be open at Ten, and the Champions mount at Twelve

Note, there will be several bye Battles as usual; particularly one between the noted Cock-Eye, from Brick-Street, and the Sailor that made so terrible a Battle the Day that the Battle Royal was fought, for Two Guineas each; and another between Tom Clintham and the Irish Boy, for a guinea each.

Gentlemen may depend upon a good Day's Diversion

This was in 1742 and it should be noted that the prize money appeared to be a side stake (for a small amount) raised by the two principals. This was by no means the typical stake, for in the same year one Chatham fought John James for 60 guineas. The influence of rich patrons must have already been operating on the sport, for stakes as high as 60 guineas could clearly not have been raised by the fighters themselves. Regular promotion came to depend almost exclusively in the next seventy years on financial backing from patrons, whether individuals or consortia.

Matches were made usually by the backers of the individual fighters. One would approach the other with a challenge, which would be accepted for a certain sum. Important fights would, as it were, make themselves. The Champion would have to face his leading challengers from time to time in order to sustain his claim to the title. Thus Pearce, and later Cribb, had to prove their worth against Jem Belcher, and backers were always ready to oblige in such circumstances.

It was in general true that with no backer there could be no fight, and Scroggins was admired for having brought himself to the top of the tree without having a backer. (Scroggy was prepared to fight for very low stakes throughout most of his career.)

In the period 1814–24 the Pugilistic Club put up purses to encourage particular fights, and the pattern of matchmaking thus changed. A man could fight for a purse without having to produce an attractive side stake. But also in this period fighters began to 'sell themselves' to both the Pugilistic Club and to private backers, by challenging other fighters, either in the press, or from the ring at the Fives Court. Those backers who liked the sound of the match were able to step in and make up the fighter's stake. The Pugilistic Club occasionally granted a purse only if a sufficient side stake were put up by the contestants (Dutch Sam v Nosworthy, etc).

It was the stake or wager which necessitated the preparation of articles of agreement for each prizefight. Such articles are exactly similar to those used in cockfighting and in cricket at the same period and they served in all three sports to establish a common practice which preceded rules or laws. The preparation of articles of agreement may seem, at first sight, surprising to those not aware of the widespread interest in sporting spectacles at the time. It was not only of interest to the principals and their patrons, but to other backers, who would not necessarily be present at a match but whose interest and confidence would only be aroused by a perusal of the articles, which were usually published, whether as handbills or in the newspapers. The articles established the stake and also the method of payment:

Ten pounds a side are deposited in the hands of Mr. Soares (President of the Daffy Club) and the remaining ten pounds to be made good at the Castle Tavern on Monday, May 29th, between the hours of seven and eleven o'clock. The forty pounds are to be placed in the hands of Mr. Jackson. Either party declining the contest to forfeit the deposit money. (Oliver v Painter in 1820)

In addition to the side stakes the Pugilistic Club at Norwich agreed to give a purse of 100 guineas, 'the purse to be placed in the hands of a Banker previous to the day of fighting'.

The articles were frequently drawn up in one of the sporting houses and if John Jackson were not nominated to hold the stake, then the landlord was often requested to undertake this office. The Castle Tavern was the most famous rendezvous and its successive landlords, Bob Gregson, Tom Belcher, or Tom Spring were called upon as stakeholder, but provincial houses were also used.

A word on the size of the stakes and the purses. There were several fights for very high stakes, in particular those between Josh Hudson and Tom Cannon for £500 a side, Tom Cribb and Molyneux (second fight) for £300 a side, Henry Pearce and John Gully for 600 guineas and 400 guineas, and Henry Pearce and Jem Belcher for 500 guineas a side. These stakes were, however, quite out of the ordinary and apart from the extraordinary sum raised for Hudson and Cannon, such high stakes were evident only in the days of the great champions—Jem Belcher, Pearce (the Game Chicken), John Gully and Tom Cribb. Cribb found it convenient to ask for £1,000 to fight Bill Neat, in order to avoid having to meet a younger and possibly dangerous opponent.

A stake of £50 a side was usual for the more important fights and many fights were arranged for much less. We have seen that the Pugilistic Club would offer a purse in addition to the side stakes, but their purses ranged between 5 and 50 guineas only. It was usual for an unknown fighter to be backed for £5 or £10 and as he gained in prestige his backing would increase, but it was most unusual to exceed £100 a side and in his latter days he might of course find he would be backed for only the lower stakes, with the occasional Club purse thrown in. It was customary for the loser to receive a collection, in addition to half the gate money. John Jackson was the best collector, particularly persuasive on behalf of a gallant loser—he obtained £50 for Molyneux after his defeat by Cribb at Thistleton Gap.

Let us return to that extraordinary promotion in 1824 for the second fight between Spring and Langan at Chichester. The articles, as was customary, had not stated the exact venue; it was simply 'to take place within 100 miles of London'. However, Mr Hewlings, feeling able to guarantee non-interference by the magistrates, nominated the place well in advance of the fight and was able to build a formidable stage—'six feet from the ground, and planked with three inch deal'.

It was always the practice to state the venue in general rather than specific terms in the articles, to allow the magistrates no opportunity of intervening. Hence the use of such phrases as 'within 100 miles of London' (Spring v Langan), 'between London and Bristol' (Spring v Neat), 'within 20 miles of the city of Norwich' (Painter v Oliver).

There were a number of venues. The most famous was Moulsey Hurst, to which point it was necessary to cross by ferry, which hazard, or logistical problem, played some part at least in keeping the magistrates away; and Moulsey was undoubtedly under the patronage of the Duke of Clarence in nearby Bushey Park.

I have analysed the venues of some 300 prizefights between 1790 and 1824 and the results give a clear indication of the pattern of prizefight venues across these years. Moulsey Hurst was not used until 22 August 1797 (Jack Bartholomew v Tom Owen) and not again until 11 March 1805, when the Game Chicken beat Elias Spray, the coppersmith. From that date fights took place there regularly and indeed there were no less than eighty-four between 1805 and 1824. The greatest number of fights in any one year was in 1821 when twelve prizefights were held at Moulsey on seven separate dates. Sixteen battles were fought between January 1816 and September 1817 in the surge of the sport's popularity following the formation of the Pugilistic Club. The Pugilistic Club undoubtedly preferred to stage its battles in the Moulsey area, for twenty-four were staged at Coombe Wood and Coombe Warren between 1814 and 1818, including ten in 1816, which was something of an *annus mirabilis* for pugilism. Coombe Wood had become popular in 1811; no fights were held there before then.

There were few fights in London itself, though there was one between Ben Brain and a Grenadier near where the British Museum now stands. But there were many fights on the London commons, and in particular at Wimbledon Common and Hyde Park. Seventeen fights took place at Wimbledon between 1788 and 1823, spread fairly evenly across the period. Indeed common ground throughout the country was popular for the promotion of fights. Twelve took place at Crawley Downs in Sussex between 1800 and 1823, including the famous fight between Randall and Martin, which ended in one round. Old Oak Common, near Highgate, witnessed twenty fights between 1810 and 1832, retaining its popularity at the close of the 1820s, when the number of fights was decreasing.

It became customary to hold fights on racecourses, which had the merit of having large grandstands available to accommodate spectators. The use of racecourses for fights other than turn-ups was a surprisingly late development: I have traced twenty-eight before 1830 and only two of these were fought before 1820.

But of course not all the famous fights took place at one of the regular venues. Johnson fought Perrins at Banbury, Humphries and Mendoza fought at Odiham in Hampshire, at Stilton in Hampshire and at Doncaster. Pearce fought Gully at Hailsham, Sussex, and Belcher at Blythe in Notts. Cribb fought Jem Belcher at Epsom Downs, and Molyneux at Copthorne Common and Thistleton Gap, Leicester. None of these places was a regular venue for prizefights any more than was Newbury, where the Gasman lost to Bill Neat.

Some of these venues seem to be very much out of the way, and indeed the more out of the way the venue perhaps the less likely to attract the magistrates. But the organisation of prizefighting was continually dogged by the problem of finding a spot which could both accommodate the crowds and yet be free from interference by the law. Some projected fights did not take place because of this difficulty.

The magistrates often appeared in person to prevent a fight. A roped ring had been prepared about a mile and a half from Twickenham to accommodate Jack Randall and West-country Dick in April 1817. Everything was ready for the fight when a gentleman rode into the ring, having all the appearance of an amateur, but who

> unfortunately, in *propria persona*, turned out to be a county magistrate. He very politely requested the official characters to remove the ring, and to disperse as soon as possible. He observed that he had been upon his horse ever since seven in the morning on the look-out and that it was morally impossible the battle could take place in Middlesex.

Certain magistrates were known as being particularly opposed to pugilism. In addition to those of Middlesex and Buckingham the magistrates of Suffolk and Cambridge harassed the fighters. Berkshire, Sussex, Kent and Surrey were less severe. It was observed by a very respectable eyewitness that the fight between White-headed Bob and Jem Burns at Twyford, near Reading, was connived at by the magistrates and police.

Lavengro described the views of one county magistrate, and there must have been many such:

> Boxing is a noble art—a truly English art; may I never see the day when Englishmen shall feel ashamed of it, or blacklegs or blackguards bring it into disgrace. I am a magistrate and, of course, cannot patronise the thing very openly, yet I sometimes see a prizefight.

Dick Christian, the great huntsman, attended the second fight between Cribb and Molyneux, and he recalled, 'all the magistrates in the county of Rutland were there. It was the Saturday magistrates' meeting at Oakham, and they all came off to the fight when they'd done—the whole kit on 'em'. However, a number of fights were stopped by magistrates and almost all were threatened.

Let us turn now to the arrangements made for the spectators at the many fights which were successfully organised. Prizefights were held in a variety of places—open fields, racecourses, inn-yards, rooms, and even prison yards.

The last fight of the series between Humphries and Mendoza was held in an innyard at Doncaster, for the benefit of subscribers who had paid half a guinea each to see the fight and a large wooden fence was erected to keep out the mob. The 500 ticket holders were, however, joined by several hundred gatecrashers, who removed the palings that were obstructing their view.

Printed tickets were unusual but they were also used for the inner ring in the fight between Cribb and Gregson at Moulsey Hurst, being printed in the colours of the fighters and sold at the sporting houses before the fight. The price was high at 3 guineas, but it was reported that 400 had been sold some days before the fight.

The gate money was more often taken literally at the gate of a field, which was the usual venue of the fights. Pugilists were often employed at the gate to assist in obtaining payment, but it is likely that a majority of spectators paid nothing.

Facilities for the spectators were often provided. Marquees had been erected to sell food and drink at Twickenham when Randall and West-country Dick were due to meet, and marquees were a regular sight at Moulsey Hurst, witness Reynolds' apostrophe:

> Behold the Hurst
> with tents encampt on't.

Such was the fear of interference by magistrates that it was rare for the organisers to be able to provide seating accommodation for any of the spectators. The normal arrangements would be the outer ring to accommodate the backers and the swells, an area for standing spectators and then a ring of waggons or carriages round the outer perimeter providing a rough sort of grandstand. The scene is familiar in many of the prints (see p 68). Dick Christian, the huntsman, watched the second Cribb v Molyneux fight at Thistleton Gap, standing on the saddle of his horse to get a better view over the vast concourse of spectators; and at Hickledown Downs when Spring fought Painter a number of spectators perched in the branches of the fir trees surrounding the ring.

Where the non-interference of magistrates could be guaranteed a wooden stage might be built for the ring, both to protect the fighters from an encroaching crowd and to afford a better view for the spectators. Also grandstands were constructed to accommodate the spectators. For the Painter v Oliver fight at North Walsham in 1820 'so little apprehension was entertained of the fight being removed that a stage of 100 yards in length was erected for spectators'. Of course, if a fight were arranged at a racecourse the ring would be built near the grandstands. Spring fought Langan at Worcester racecourse on 7 January 1824 and it was estimated that 30,000 were present. The figure of 30,000 spectators quoted here is not surprising, though there was no way of recording an accurate gate, as many of the spectators were not ticket holders. The numbers recorded by eyewitnesses as watching the fights is of interest, however: 30,000 were also said to have watched Spring v Neat at Hinckley Down near Andover (1823), and Carter v Oliver at Carlisle (1816); and 20,000 Carter v Robinson at Moulsey Hurst (1816). Accurate or not, these figures can be taken as confirming that prizefights were almost invariably attended by large crowds—'a Roman carnival was not half so hearty a thing as a prizefight used to be when the people's hearts were in it'.

Certainly it was a matter of comment if the crowds were small. There were 'not above 600 persons present' to see Randall fight Holt in 1817; and the editor of *The Fancy Gazette* reported that 'not more than a thousand persons watched Tom Shelton fight

Josh Hudson' in 1822 and used this 'paucity of numbers' as a text to preach a sermon on the poor state of the sport, with its crossed fights, etc. William Windham attended one fight where there was a small crowd and recorded:

> Nothing could be more unlike a meeting for such a purpose (prizefighting) in the neighbourhood of London. No great crowd, no traffic of people hurrying along the road, nothing that could be called tumult; it was . . . more like a congregation of Puritans assembled to hear one of Cromwell's preachers.

The crowds were all male, it being a matter for carnival when females attended the second Randall–Martin fight and the Randall–Turner epic. The composition of the crowds is interesting and it seems evident that the majority would be local inhabitants. The venue was not announced in advance, but a crowd of the Fancy passing through a country area was evidence enough of what was afoot. In times when public entertainment was scarce, a prizefight, like a fair or the local races, would attract enormous local interest. This is shown in an anecdote by a man who was to become mayor of Reading and who was not an advocate of prizefighting. He attended the fight between White-headed Bob and Jem Burns at Twyford in 1827 and he describes how he came to be present:

> With a friend, I was driving through Twyford on our way to keep an appointment at Knowl Hill, but seeing several carriages and many persons on foot going towards Ruscombe Lake, which is near Twyford, we found on enquiry that they were on their way to see a Prize Fight between two celebrated Boxers. Up to that moment neither of us had any idea that a contest of this kind was about to occur.

This would be the way with most of the crowd, swept along to the excitement of watching something unusual. Many, in fact, did not go to watch two men fighting, but to see a public spectacle. Of course a part of the crowd consisted of the 'regulars', the 'family' of the London Fancy. Such men were in the know as to the venues of the fights and travelled out of London to see all they could. They included gentlemen and the hard-core Fancy, those inhabitants of the sporting world who lived with a new intensity when a fight and a bet were in prospect. The venue of a fight could be ascertained the day before by enquiry at any of the sporting houses favoured by the Fancy.

The organisers of prizefights did not hold themselves responsible for the behaviour of the crowds attracted by the fights. For obvious reasons they could not ask for the assistance of constables in controlling the crowds, but they were anxious to control the crowds sufficiently to enable the fight to be completed without the ring being broken, whether by design, or simply by the pressure of a vast multitude. To this end pugilists were engaged to patrol the area of the outer ring and beat out the ring before the fight.

One final point on organisation. Generally, there was just one fight on the bill, but there were nevertheless many occasions when there were one or two supporting bouts. This became more common when the Pugilistic Club became involved in the organisation. In a modern promotion the top of the bill is usually the last fight, but it was more often first in days when the law might break up a meeting at any time.

The Times of 17 August 1804 described the background to one fight:

It has been for some time known that a battle between Pittoon [Bitton] the Jew, and Wood the coachman was to be fought. . . . The vigilance of the magistrates around the Metropolis has lately been so great to prevent scenes of this kind taking place, that much caution was used to keep secret the time and place of the contest. It was not until Sunday night that Wilsdon Green was named.

The main fight came first and Bitton beat Wood. 'Several other battles were about to be fought but the arrival of the Bow Street officers prevented them.'

G

CHAPTER SIX

The Fight

I've watched the seconds pat and nurse
Their man; and seen him put to bed;
With twenty guineas in his purse,
And not an eye within his head.

                    J. H. Reynolds: *The Fancy*

The published rules of prizefighting, such as they were, remained virtually unaltered for a century. In 1743 several gentlemen agreed a set of rules to be observed in all battles fought at Jack Broughton's amphitheatre. These rules became accepted as the basis for almost all prizefights in the succeeding century until the 'New Rules' of 1838. But for each fight articles of agreement were drawn up and the fights reflected customary practice, which evolved over a number of years. The articles were concerned with questions of money, the stake, the stakeholder, the amount of deposit, etc, but they also detailed matters relating to the actual battle itself. They stated, for example, the size of the ring—a matter on which Broughton's rules had made no pronouncement. We shall see how greatly the ring sizes differed. The articles would usually specify the type of ring, eg, whether turf or a stage, and they occasionally dealt with the particular activities of the seconds during a fight and the restrictions of certain blows— eg, butting. It was sometimes stated that 'a man must not go down without a blow' (Mendoza v Humphries 1789 and Gully v Gregson 1807).

It will be seen that these particular articles assumed an agreed code of practice in the prizering. This was based on Broughton's rules, but there were also unwritten rules, as one particular fight will show: in the tenth round of the fight between Ned Turner and Jack Randall, Turner complained that Randall had trod heavily upon his toe and said 'Do you call that fair, Jack?' Randall denied that he had done so, and implicit in his denial was the fact that such an act would have been unfair. Edmund Burke had declared that 'Nations are not primarily ruled by laws'. Rather they are ruled by conventions, which make formal laws comparatively infrequent. This was certainly true of prizefighting in the era to which Burke referred.

In the 'New Rules' of 1838 the size of the ring was finally declared to be 'four and twenty feet square'. Broughton's rules had not specified a size and there had been a variety of ring measurements. Tom Cribb beat Jem Belcher at Moulsey Hurst in 1807 in a 20ft square ring. In the return fight on Epsom racecourse in 1809 they fought in a ring 30ft square. When Cribb beat Molyneux in the first of their legendary fights, at Copthorne Common in 1810, the match was made in a ring 24ft square. Big Ben Brain who was to beat Tom Johnson in a 20ft ring in a battle for the title of Champion in 1790 had previously beaten Corbally the Irish chairman in a ring 25ft square (1788). Dutch Sam, the great Jewish lightweight, fought one of the few draws in the history of prizefighting against Tom Belcher in 1807 at Moulsey Hurst in a 28ft square ring, whereas the third of their fights took place in a 30ft ring. Those three fights, incidentally, were acclaimed by the Fancy, as Tom Belcher, brother of the champion Jem, was the most skilful and stylish of boxers, while the Jew was considered the greatest fighter pound for pound the prizering had yet seen. There were some few fights in rings 40ft square (Jack Ford v Davis at Redmarley in Gloucestershire, Gully and Gregson in 1808 and Tom Belcher v Warr, junior, in

1804). The smallest ring I know of was 18ft square, and it was used for the contest between Bill Warr and Wood in 1795. The largest, 48ft square, was used for one of the fights between Humphries and Mendoza.

The New Rules stated exactly how the ring should be contained 'with eight stakes and ropes'—there being two ropes, the higher 4ft from the ground. Broughton's rules had not stated this matter specifically and there had been a wide divergence of 'markers'. Not only were ropes used, but planks and poles and also the straightforward congress of men where the front row marked the boundary of the ring. Stakes and ropes were the most common but Tom Johnson beat Isaac Perrins, the Birmingham giant, in 1787 in a ring which was 'railed in' with wood. The evidence of prints is particularly interesting with regard to the make-up of the ring. In his *National Sports*, published in 1820, Henry Alken showed his fighters contending in a ring with a single rope, a good deal lower than 4ft. (Alken prints in this volume were normally accurate representations.) In a mezzotint by Charles Turner after an oil by Douglas Guest painted in 1811 we see Cribb setting-to in a ring with a single plank boundary. The roped ring with two lines of ropes can be seen in a popular print by Robert Cruikshank of the fight between Jack Randall (the 'Nonpareil') and Martin (the 'Master of the Rolls') in 1821 (see bookjacket). The many engravings in *Boxiana* reveal a variety of retainers, though mostly ropes. In two prints by Rowlandson the men fight with spectators forming the ring; this was not necessarily artistic licence, for when O'Donnel fought Harry Holt at Moulsey Hurst in 1816 'the ring was kept in good order, altho' no stakes and ropes were used to protect the men from the crowd'.

There are interesting prints of the Fives Court in St Martin's Lane, where regular sparring exhibitions took place—usually before the gentlemen of the Fancy for the benefit of a pugilist. Turner's engraving after Blake shows a roped ring. Alken's print has wood rails. In a Cruikshank print (p 151) the ring has a wood rail and in another by the same artist it has wooden poles tied to the stakes.

The evidence points to a variety of different sorts of ring, but the roped ring came to predominate; one reason was that a great number were made by one man, Bill Gibbons, and his rings were usually made with stakes and ropes. Indeed, as we have seen, in 1814 when the Pugilistic Club was formed, Gibbons was appointed ringmaker and was provided with ropes and stakes, the stakes being eight in number and 'capped and shod with iron, distinguished at the tops with the letters "P.C." '. Even here it should be noted that the PC ring was 20ft square with three ropes in the early days, becoming 24ft later.

The stakes varied in height and could be dangerous. In his fight against Tom Spring in 1818 Ned Painter fell and 'the back of his head and part of his shoulder came into violent contact against one of the stakes'. The unfortunate Painter lost to Cribb's young protégé as a result. When Pierce Egan supervised the erection of a ring he ensured that 'the angular sides of the rails were planed round'. Certainly more care was taken with the stakes but the ropes used were also the cause of damage in fights where wrestling and clinching were not forbidden. In a fight between Jem Burns and White-headed Bob at Twyford in 1823 we are told by an eyewitness that both fighters 'fell against the ropes, and were dreadfully punished by their backs being so badly cut'. On another occasion Josh Hudson got his head caught in the ropes and his opponent took the opportunity of playing upon it like a drum until he slid to the floor.

The floor of the ring merits some examination. The 'New Rules' of 1838 specified a turf ring but there had always been a variety of surfaces. As almost every fight was held in the open air the ring floor was open to the elements. Moreover, there was no close season, fights taking place throughout the year. Turf floors, natural grass, were of course the most common, but after rain grass could and often did turn to mud. When Jack Martin fought Sampson in 1820 there was heavy rain and 'the Master of the

Rolls, slipped about all over the ring, as if he had been sliding on a pond'. Sometimes, when the grass was sodden, sawdust was used (Sampson v Belasco). Shelton fought Oliver in January and the men stripped and fought on sawdust-covered snow.

An alternative base to the ring was wooden boards. This was not a late introduction, having been known since the days of Broughton's amphitheatre. Tom Johnson lost his title to Ben Brain on a wooden stage in 1790 and in the same year Mendoza won the third of his battles with Gentleman Humphries on a wooden stage raised 4ft from the ground. Wooden floors were not proof against rain. Gentleman Jackson lost to George Inglesden, the 'brewer', in 1789 when he broke his leg because of the slippery state of the stage. There is an excellent picture of a wooden stage in a mezzotint of Cribb after Guest. When Hudson and Cannon fought at Warwick in 1824 a wooden stage was erected under the immediate direction of Pierce Egan. *Boxiana* describes it:

> It was six feet from the ground, supported by eight substantial posts, and the upper rail was four feet three inches above the surface. There was a narrow shelving skirting board at the bottom, to prevent the heads of the men from coming into contact with the edges of the boards.

Even these rather unusual precautions could not prevent Hudson's head 'rebounding by the force of the fall' as he was knocked unconscious. One last point. There were stages built of turf. On such a surface Tom Johnson defeated the giant Perrins.

The organisers of prizefights were ever conscious of the ring break-up and it was the regular practice to build two rings, the inner ring and the outer ring. The inner ring was, of course, for the pugilists and the four seconds, who remained in the ring with the pugilists. The outer ring was basically a crowd-break but was occupied by the two umpires and the referee and by the backers and their particular friends. And 'between the rings the swells were accommodated for a quid each'. The job of patrolling the outer ring fell to the lot of professional pugilists. In 1817 four famous pugilists fought an unavailing battle to keep the ring clear when Scroggins fought Turner, being overwhelmed by perhaps the unruliest mob in the history of prizefighting. An estimated crowd of 30,000 was present and public order entirely broke down.

To clear the outer ring before the main battle started was called 'beating out' the ring. This was quite literally beating anyone who had no claim to be there with sticks, fists, or horse-whips. Clearly the men to do this were professional fighters and equally clearly their activities would be resented by those to whom they applied their professional skill. Caleb Baldwin, the leary old champion of Westminster, bought himself a tartar when he struck a young coloured boy. The youth, named Bristow, gave old Caleb a couple of facers that covered his face with blood. Needless to say, young Bristow was persuaded to exhibit his spirit for reward in the prizering itself. However well patrolled the outer ring was, there was no preventing the actions of men such as those recorded by Squire Osbaldeston, who was referee-ing a fight at Newmarket at which some ruffians kept throwing sods at the umpires. One hit him on the head, but, says the Squire, 'my hat saved it'.

The chucker-out is rarely a popular figure. For fights held under the auspices of the Pugilistic Club the attendants wore dark blue ribbons in their hats to distinguish them so that no one was likely to make the mistake of assaulting the wrong man! The apogee of the trade of ring attendant was undoubtedly when George IV employed a number of prizefighters to guard the exterior of Westminster Hall during his coronation.

Rule 3 of the 1838 Rules specified what had become the accepted custom—that each fighter should have a coloured hand-kerchief, that these 'colours' should be intertwined on one of the stakes, and that the winner should claim both. This practice had grown up since Tom Johnson in the 1780s had introduced the practice of wearing colours, his own being sky blue. But it was Jem Belcher who popularised the wearing of colours and indeed

gave his name to the 'yellowman' or 'Belcher', and successive
Bristolians adopted this colour—Jem's brother Tom, John Gully
and Bill Neat. Not only were the colours tied to the ropes; the
fighters held up their drawers with a tie of their own colours, and
their drawers were tied below the knee with a coloured garter.
The seconds and the bottlemen wore the colours as scarves and
belts. The colours were tied one over the other on one of the
stakes or the ropes and there are instances of a colour being
untied and thrown in as a sign of surrender—of throwing in the
towel. When Scroggins fought Turner in 1817, Scroggins' second
'hoisted up the handkerchief as a token of defeat'.

It was traditional for the winner to wear the loser's handkerchief after the fight and little account was paid to the feelings of
the loser as the victor was driven to town in triumph wearing the
spoils of victory. In the famous over-age match in 1820 in which
Tom Owen, aged 51, met Mendoza, aged 55, Owen won and
'soon returned to the ring decorated in all the paraphernalia
attendant upon conquest . . . poor Dan's blue trophy was hung
carelessly round Owen's neck'. But when the popular Irish
champion Dan Donnelly beat Oliver in 1819,

> on quitting his room to enter the apartment of Oliver the
> coloured handkerchief which he had won, belonging to his fallen
> opponent, he would not publicly wear by way of exultation, or to
> wound the feelings of Oliver, but concealed it by way of pad, in
> the green handkerchief which he wore round his own neck.

It seems that not only was it the practice of the winner to sport
his antagonist's colours, but on occasion the loser would acknowledge defeat by wearing his conqueror's colours. When Oliver
was thrashed by Painter 'after resting himself upon his second's
knee for about a minute, he dressed himself and put the yellow
handkerchief round his neck'. The current practice of jersey-
swopping in a number of sports perhaps reflects the precedent.

The handkerchiefs, or fogles, were of silk and were made at
Spitalfields, London, which had an immigrant population that
had brought the art of silk preparation from Holland. Not only

did the fighters and their attendants sport their colours but so did their supporters. When Henry Pearce defeated Jem Belcher in 1803 and won the title of Champion

> that handkerchief which had so long been the fashion (à la Belcher) in gracing the bosoms of some of our most elevated and beautiful countrywomen, and which had, likewise, so often formed a part of the dress of the successful partisans, in compliment to their favourite hero, was at length placed in a secondary point of view—but in losing its situation, let it never be forgotten . . . that its colour remained unsullied.

Fighters did not always retain the same colours. Tom Owen adopted the 'yellowman' as a result of defeating 'Bully' Hooper, the 'Tinman'. It seems that Scroggins changed his colours after seven successful fights and Josh Hudson used at least three different colours. When Langan met Spring it was a case of black and blue, which accurately reflected two of the most bruising fights the prizering had seen. What would happen if two men with the same colours met? Probably one would change. Henry Pearce as a Bristol man would have been expected to sport a yellowman but because Belcher the champion was also a yellowman Pearce sported a blue-spotted handkerchief. There was an amusing diversion at the fight in 1823 between Shelton and Josh Hudson when the colours which had been affixed to the stakes were stolen.

The pugilists stripped to the waist for their fights and as these took place throughout the year there was often the danger of chill either during or after a fight. Poor Jack Power's constitution was undermined in his last fight against Jack Carter, when the weather affected him so seriously 'that for several hours his frame did not experience the least warmth whatever. His blood was so chilled that animation appeared nearly suspended'. Fortunately the doctors succeeded in removing 'the frigid oppressor from his person', but Power never really recovered, and died shortly afterwards. Molyneux, coming from Virginia, had not accustomed himself to the English climate when he first fought Cribb. After getting on top he was seized with a violent shivering fit and seemed to collapse.

The fighters usually changed in the barouche in which they came to the ground. It would have been more convenient in a nearby inn but the innkeeper could have been accused of aiding and abetting a breach of the peace. Before retreating to the barouche to strip, it was the custom for the pugilists to throw their hat into the ring as a token of defiance, and incidentally to inform their opponent and the spectators that they had arrived. There was a curious incident when Brown (the 'Sprig of Myrtle') met Dick Curtis (the 'Pet of the Fancy') in 1820. 'Brown threw his hat in the ring, but the wind blew it out; shortly afterwards Curtis repeated the act of defiance, but the wind also blew his white topper out of the ring. This was a *tye* upon the bad omen.'

The hat was thrown in on occasion, like the coloured handkerchief and the sponge as a token of defeat. When Tom Oliver could not answer the call of time against Painter his second 'threw in the hat' and victory was proclaimed for Painter.

A word about the *scratch*. The fighters had to come up to the *mark* or *scratch* at the beginning of the fight and at the expiry of the half-minute break. This ruling did not change, save only that the 'New Rules' of 1838 insisted that the fighter should come to the scratch unaided by his seconds. Before the round began both fighters had to take up their positions at the scratch in the centre of the ring. This made for the setpiece of taking up the stance which distinguishes the old style of prizefighting from our own. The pugilists were not allowed to begin fighting until they had positioned themselves, rather like the setting-to of fighting dogs or cocks. It was felt necessary that the start of each round should preserve exact equality and seconds were not slow to complain if a round began without the formality.

After the seconds had tossed (in *Fancyana* Bee says this practice began in 1802), the winner chose his corner according to the state of the wind or sun, and conducted his man thereto, the loser taking the opposite corner. There were clear advantages to be gained from winning the toss in certain conditions. In 1819 Turner lost the toss against Martin 'but seldom failed by his manoeuvres to place his adversary with his face to the sun'. Perhaps Turner had picked up the trick from his fight with Randall the previous year when the latter 'got Turner in the sun and put in a tremendous hit on his left side'.

The selection and duties of the umpires and the referee did not change significantly. Timekeeping was of course restricted to the half-minute interval after which the man must come up to the scratch. The rounds lasted until a man, or indeed both men, were knocked or thrown off their feet. A round could, therefore, last a few seconds or much longer. The fact that a fight lasted for 50 rounds does not itself reveal the length of time for which it was contested. It would be meaningless to state an average time a round lasted but it can be said that 30 rounds would probably take about 1hr including the intervals. Even this could be mis-leading as one or two examples show. Two Midlanders, Griffiths and Baylis, fought 213 ROUNDS in the space of 4hr ½min. In contrast, when Molyneux fought Fuller in 1814 the first round continued for 28min and 'in sixty eight minutes only two rounds had taken place'. This last was certainly exceptional and it was considered a matter for comment when Randall and Belasco fought only 7 rounds in 54½min—the first round lasting 9min. If the fighters maintained a high level of activity, such as a modern referee would insist upon, the round could be expected to be short. When Painter and Oliver milled each other, 'it excited the greatest surprise in the most experienced pugilists' that a round lasted for more than 2min.

The umpire's timekeeping duties then were restricted to the intervals when thirty seconds had long been accepted as the time after which a man must come up to the scratch. The umpires, though each side appointed one, were expected to be impartial and they were usually chosen from among the *gentlemen*, whereas the seconds were almost always ex-fighters. Those who acted as umpires included Sir Thomas Apreece, Captain Barclay,

Colonel Barton, Lord Yarmouth, and that most ubiquitous sportsman, Squire Osbaldeston. The umpires did not always call upon a third to act as referee, though by the end of the eighteenth century this had become accepted practice and 'Gentleman' Jackson was normally invited to occupy that office in any fight which he attended. There being few rules as to the method of fighting, the umpires were rarely called upon to act in a capacity other than that of timekeeper. But there were exceptions and several of these drew attention to the need for a referee to adjudicate not only between the fighters but also the umpires. In the second of his three fights with Humphries in 1789 Mendoza had Sir Thomas Apreece as his umpire. In the twenty-second round Humphries fell without a blow, which was contrary to the articles of agreement for this fight. Mendoza's umpire, therefore, declared it to be a foul, but Humphries' umpire would not agree. An appeal was then made to Mr Coombe 'who would not decide upon the case'. In the third fight a man of stronger character— Colonel Harvey Aston—was appointed as referee.

To be a referee you had to be made of pretty stern stuff. Squire Osbaldeston, who was referee in four fights, recalled:

> The referee's office is always a thankless one . . . for the partisans of the combatants are constantly appealing to the referee, crying 'Foul!' etc. particularly when they see their man getting the worst of it. Whatever your decision may be, one party is sure to accuse the referee of partiality, and they actually give him notice not to part with the stakes, threatening legal proceedings if he does. 'Wrangle, Tie or Win' is their creed, to save their money, not caring sixpence for the sufferings of either man.

By the very nature of prizefighting the winner was usually clearly seen; there were no points decisions. But it was obviously necessary to establish that in cases of dispute the decision of the umpires and the referee should be final. The ruling was stated clearly by Gentleman Jackson in a letter written in December 1814 to the *Morning Post* after doubts had been raised as to the result of a fight between Nosworthy and Dutch Sam.

Sir, In answer to the statement which has this day appeared in your journal, I must be permitted to observe that no decision can properly be given on the subject of any pugilistic contest, except by the umpires appointed on such occasions. Whatever debate may exist with regard to the conduct of Dutch Sam in his late encounter with Nosworthy, must be referred to the three gentlemen who preside in that capacity. I am not aware of any meeting to set aside the bets without their concurrence.

The umpires were also the arbiters on such questions as the division of the gate money on the rare occasions when it was not divided equally.

The umpires and the referee were usually stationed in the outer ring, or immediately next to the ring when a stage was built. On one occasion, when a stage was erected, a small platform was raised for the accommodation of the umpires and referee, their heads coming in line with the feet of the men. There is a rather macabre story about an unusually officious umpire in the second Randall–Martin fight. Poor Martin was lying unconscious when this umpire addressed him: 'Martin, I must remind you this is a stand-up fight'.

We must now examine the activities of the seconds in more detail. Two men were allowed to each fighter, the *kneeman* and the *bottleman*, though their roles were interchangeable. The kneeman would provide his knee for his man to sit on during the intervals between rounds—the stool not being introduced until later in the nineteenth century. The bottleman had the bottle, the sponge and the orange. Whether the bottle contained water or 'prime jackey' was left to the predilections of the fighter or to his seconds. A flask of brandy would be carried for emergencies as its reviving powers were much appreciated; when the indomitable Jack Scroggins was hit down by Ned Turner 'brandy was called for to renovate the little hero'. The resort to spirits to revive a man as demonstrated by the professional cornerman had unfortunate effects on a boy at Eton in 1825. We know that the boys followed the activities of the prizering with the closest attention, and on one occasion their eager emulation of professional practice had disastrous results. Ashley Minimus, one of Lord Shaftesbury's sons, was in a fight against a bigger boy. In the middle of the fight Ashley 'drank half a pint of brandy, which was too much for him, and after renewing the fight for some time afterwards, he fainted and died in consequence of the brandy and the blows on his temples'. At the inquest Ashley Major said that his brother would not have been able to stand up and fight had he not been given the brandy. In further explanation he said that he had advised his brother only to wash his mouth with it, but the boy had drunk the whole bottle!

The professional cornermen used ardent spirits more discreetly on their man, but there is one incident which might suggest that they were not unwilling to drink the same medicine. When Scroggins fought Turner for the second time, his second, Clark, fell down in a fit during the eighteenth round; but it is pleasing to learn that 'it did not interrupt the fight; he was instantly taken away and proper means used for his recovery'. In one of his early fights Tom Cannon had to attend his own second, who was 'three sheets in the wind'.

The seconds' principal work was to get their man fit to answer the call of 'time' after the half-minute interval. In addition to their bottle they had a sponge, which served a dual purpose, being employed to wipe a man's brow and douse him with cold water. It was also used as the sign of defeat: when their man could not be set at the mark the handlers would throw in the sponge. This acknowledgement was much more common than throwing in the colours, mentioned above.

Some seconds were more ready to throw in the sponge than others. Tom Owen was said to be one of the finest of seconds and a man who did not drag his man half conscious to the scratch; and old Joe Norton, master of ceremonies at the Fives Court, who was a regular second, was 'a most attentive and humane man in his attendance upon a losing pugilist. . . . His exertions on behalf of one pugilist he was attending were rewarded by a small subscription being collected for him in respect of his humane conduct'. Tom Belcher was rather of the other school, not owning his man to be beaten until he was totally insensible. Bill Wood was a second in the Tom Belcher mould. When his man, Dutch Sam, declared he could fight no longer, Wood quickly clapped a handkerchief on his mouth and would not let him speak.

Rule 10 of the 1838 rules states that 'the seconds shall not interfere, advise or direct the adversary of their principal, and shall refrain from all offensive and irritating expressions'. That such a rule was necessary can be seen from the appalling behaviour of the former champion Tom Johnson when acting as second to Richard Humphries in his first fight against Daniel Mendoza.

> During the whole time of the battle . . . he was abusing Mendoza, and looking him in the face, in order to take away his attention from his adversary, and even at one critical period of the combat, when Humphrey's loins were exposed and Mendoza was about sticking into his kidneys, a stroke which must have terminated the battle, he (Johnson) stepped in between them and stopped the blow.

Broughton himself said that 'in *his* time, he [Johnson] would have been kicked off the stage'. The 1838 rules would also have caused Johnson's dismissal from the ring, but in fact, in 1789, no action was taken against him.

A last word on the second's activities should go to a man who helped his principal's opponent rather than performed his rightful duty. The second was Tom Tring, the Prince of Wales' former favourite, and he was seconding Mendoza in his fight against Martin 'the Bath Butcher' in 1789. The *Morning Herald* in describing the fight recorded 'it is remarkable that Tring twice supported Martin who would otherwise have fallen to the ground, which was at length noticed by Mendoza, who knocked him off the stage'. One can scarcely blame Mendoza for his hasty action but I would prefer to believe that it was a momentary aberration by Tring rather than a deliberate action by a second whose money was on the other man. This last was a not uncommon occurrence, but Tring seconded Mendoza in several of his later fights and was still appearing as a second as late as December 1800 (Jem Belcher v Gamble).

I have dealt in chapter seven with the customary technique practised by the fighters. Here I will draw attention to some of their malpractices. It was clearly unsatisfactory that a man should go down without a blow at the beginning of a round, thus gaining for himself a full minute's respite (ie, two half-minute intervals). Indeed it was regularly forbidden in the articles of agreement (Humphries v Mendoza, Gully v Gregson, etc). There was, however, no way in which this sort of situation could be avoided if a man dropped to his knees after a blow which was not itself a *knock-down* blow. Who was to say whether it was not a blow from which a man should have fallen? It would depend on the length of the battle (rounds generally became shorter the longer the fight lasted), the condition of the man, whether or not he was off balance or his muscles slack at the time the blow fell. To the spectator short rounds were of little interest, and the three-minute round with the ten-second knock-down rule have given the advantage to the spectator and not to the weary fighter. The fact that more fights were not protracted by constant intervals is due to the spirit of the men who fought. Men would scarcely engage in bare-knuckle fights if they were cowards or gamesmen.

Rules 13 to 17 of the 1838 rules detail all the forbidden fouls. They replace the single rule of 1743 which said that 'no person is to hit his adversary when he is down, or seize him by the ham, the breeches or any part below the waist'. The new rules endorse the old rule and make fouls of butting, kicking, gouging, biting, tearing the flesh and falling on a man with the knees. Such actions seem manifestly unfair, as they did to the majority of protagonists before the 1838 rules spelled them out, but nevertheless they were employed often enough to make it essential to ban their use specifically. And there were other practices which the 1838 rules should perhaps have banned. One such was pulling an opponent's hair, not only causing extreme pain, but assisting in pulling a man on to a punch, which a modern referee would certainly not tolerate, however it is done. The most famous exponent of hair pulling was Gentleman John Jackson himself, who employed this ungentlemanly tactic when taking the title of Champion from the long-haired Daniel Mendoza. *The Times* gave the following brief note of the fight:

> Yesterday a Prize Battle was fought at Hornchurch in Essex between Mendoza the Jew and one Jackson, a publican of Gray's Inn Lane, when, *as had no doubt been previously settled*, the Jew appeared overpowered by the strength of the Christian.

Jackson retired from the prizering after this fight and became the most respected figure in the boxing world. Poor Mendoza had to make do with the time-honoured and salutory advice, 'Get your hair cut'.

In his third fight against Bourke, Jem Belcher kept laughing and talking to his opponent 'but not forgetting to put in severe hits'. It was said that 'in his social hours Jem was good natured in the extreme; modest and unassuming to a degree almost bordering upon bashfulness'. Such a thing could never be said of Dutch Sam, whether inside or outside the ring. In his fight against Britton, Sam behaved in a most singular fashion. Holding up his hands in the air he suggested his opponent wanted to kiss. Having knocked Britton down Sam got down on the ground alongside him and told him what he would do to him when he got up. Such gamesmanship was never against the rules, apart from those of decency and sportsmanship. When Belcher threw Bourke, 'very honourably, he fell upon his hands with an intent not to hurt Bourke any more by falling on him, which practice is not unusual and consistent with fair fighting'. This was so and the man who was thrown could expect to receive the full weight of his opponent upon him.

Tripping was, of course, allowed, as it was usually part of a throw. Turner was cheered 'for neatly tripping up Scroggins'.

H

Standing on a man's foot was not barred but it was accepted that to do this deliberately was wrong. Butting was not illegal until 1838 but when Spring fought Carter in 1819, the conduct of Carter created great disapprobation. 'It seemed as if he were fighting a bear rather than a man', for he continued to 'run in sharply with his head into Spring's body'.

Holding and hitting was perfectly in order—the head held in chancery under the arm while the other fist pounded the opponent into insensibility. This splendidly simple tactic was used not only in the prizering itself. In *Romany Rye* the jockey tells Romany Rye how he begged Miss Berners to give him a hair from her head. When she refused he tried to snatch one, when 'up she started and gave me the only dubbing I ever had in my life. Lor how, with her right hand she fibbed me whilst she held me round the neck with her left arm; I was soon glad to beg her pardon on my knees'.

There does seem to be much evidence to support the view that the organisation of prizefights was designed to prolong the spectacle for as long as possible. The half-minute rest on a knockdown saved a fighter from further immediate punishment, but it also enabled him to continue to fight for round after bloody round. Often the fights degenerated into a pushing and shoving match between two bleeding and exhausted fighters, urged on of course by the yells of their seconds and backers. The art and science of self-defence disappeared in the early stages of most fights and audience appreciation was reserved for blood and bottom. While a Regency crowd might be thought to have a stronger stomach for this debased excitement, one has only to go to a current boxing promotion to see that it is not the boxing skill but the elemental qualities of bravery and blood that really rouse the crowds.

CHAPTER SEVEN

Technique, Training and Teachers

Just like a black eye in a recent scuffle
(For sometimes we must box without the muffle.)
BYRON: *Don Juan*

There was considerable development in technique from the days
when Broughton opened his amphitheatre in 1743 to the time
when Jackson closed his rooms in Bond Street in 1824. This
development was a continuing process but certain men stand out
as initiators and the skill of others in certain manoeuvres led to
imitation by other fighters. The Fives Court exhibitions led to
the acceptance of standards of style which men like that irre-
pressible tearaway Jack Scroggins condemned as unmanly. But
the times had passed Jack by and he was a lone voice ignored by

those who wanted their bloodletting to be accompanied by a little finesse.

Captain Godfrey, writing in 1747, gives us a clear picture of Broughton's style, which was, of course, widely adopted by his contemporaries:

> He steps not back, distrusting of himself to stop a blow and piddle in the return, with an arm unaided by his body, producing but a kind of fly-flap blows. . . . No, Broughton steps bold and firmly in, bids a welcome to the coming blow, receives it with the guardian arm; then with a general summons of his swelling muscles and his firm body seconding his arm and supplying it with all his weight pours the pile-driving force upon his man.

Not only is this a vivid impression of one pugilist but it is also accurate with regard to the technique of the pugilists of Broughton's time. The normal practice of defensive boxing was 'never to shift' and to try to ward off the blows with the arms without the aid of footwork.

But after Broughton's time, and contemporary with his successor Slack, there came a fighter whose technique astonished his contemporaries and, it would be fair to say, appalled many used to the solid virtues of the Broughton school. The innovator was a lightweight named Hunt, who at 5ft 4½in and around 9 stone found himself usually overmatched physically. Making a virtue of necessity, Hunt used his feet both when defending and when leading. His tactics were called 'shifting' and they were not generally adopted because they were considered to be not quite manly. He was years ahead of his time and made no impression on the style of his contemporaries; it was in later years that he was remembered as an important figure in the history of technique.

With Mendoza's arrival the old school of boxing reached its peak in that he was distinguished for his mastery of the established skills. No man up to that time had united the theory of sparring with the practice of boxing as successfully as he. What seems sure is that Mendoza introduced to the sport nothing new except his supreme proficiency.

Up to and including Mendoza's day, then, it was the pattern of fighting for both men to take up the position or stance at the scratch, throw punches until they closed, then wrestle to throw each other with a trip or a cross-buttock. The stance was considered to be important, and indeed when the opponent's blows were thrown from a more or less predictable angle, the arms were enabled to ward off much of their force. To a modern eye the stance assumed by the pugilists, and illustrated in the countless prints of the times, seems forced and unnatural; but we must remember that, apart from the classical overtones inherent in most of the illustrations, the pugilist was guarding against an attack unlike that which the modern fighter would expect. The direction of attack was more or less predictable and it must also be appreciated that a man was permitted to grasp and pull his opponent, not only punch him.

Around 1800 the fights became less static and also more scientific. Wellington recognised the difference in style when he used a pugilistic metaphor to describe the Battle of Waterloo to Viscount Beresford a month afterwards:

> Never did I see such a pounding match. Both were what the boxers call gluttons. Napoleon did not manoeuvre at all. He just moved forward in the old style . . . and was driven off in the old style.

As often, in the history of boxing, the new style came from the Champion, and in this case it was Jem Belcher. Jem, being a force of nature, was not strictly imitable; he moved faster round his opponent and threw more punches than any of his predecessors. He was in fact little more than a middleweight and hence usually smaller than his opponents. Not unlike Hunt, forty years before, he made a virtue of his slighter build by 'springing backwards and forwards with a celerity that was truly astonishing'. To his contemporaries Jem seemed unbeatable, and even after he had lost an eye and was in poor health he was still heavily backed against Cribb. After Jem Belcher a number of other fighters made their own contributions to the development of the techniques of fighting—all, in their way, making the fight an altogether faster affair than it had been for the previous fifty years.

Bill Richmond was said to be unrivalled in the art of hitting and getting away, and was constantly on the move. At the age of 50 he could still be backed for half an hour against the best of the younger school, as he continued to demonstrate at the Fives Court. Tom Cribb was a much bigger and slower man than either Richmond or Belcher but he also moved about the ring, 'milling on the retreat'. Basically Cribb was a counterpuncher, prepared to give ground in order to seek out an opening. He was a good stopper and, though not a fast puncher, he was strong and accurate.

Two lightweights, contemporaries of Cribb and Richmond, were contributing to the new techniques: they were Dutch Sam and Tom, the younger brother of the former champion Jem Belcher. Dutch Sam is credited with introducing the uppercut, an effective blow in the sort of mauling clinch which was common in the early fights. Closing, which had been a feature of all fights in the eighteenth century, was soon to be less common now there were successful counter-measures. By 1818 Egan could say: 'Closing has for some time been exploded; and this alone may serve as an argument to show that boxing is greatly improved since what was formerly of great utility is now esteemed unnecessary or of little value'.

The role of the Fives Court in advancing the education of both fighters and spectators is discussed in chapter eight, but it was there that Tom Belcher's skills were seen to the best advantage. His manner of setting-to was admitted to be 'truly pleasing and eminent. It is not only showy but effective, and there is nothing coarse or affected about it. In this particular he almost stands alone'. And there remained few who could feint and commit an opponent to a punch as could Belcher.

Of course the old style of closing, rushing, hugging, etc, did not disappear overnight. Jack Scroggins and the 'Gasman', for example, both rushed their opponents, relying upon their strength and courage to prevail. This usually proved successful, since both men were particularly brave, but the virtues of scientific boxing were given conclusive demonstration in 1822 when Bill Neat jabbed and hooked Hickman into insensibility at Newbury in that most famous of fights.

The virtues of the straight left had been appreciated since the days of Broughton, but as the sport developed, the variety of punches increased, and in particular, a greater number of punches were thrown. Jack Randall's left hand could be likened to a hasty footman knocking impatiently at a door.

Two practices lasted from the early days of pugilism until 1841, when Vincent Dowling summed up the techniques of fighting in *Fistiana*. These were the 'suit in chancery' and the 'cross-buttock'. Both are more redolent of the early method of fighting than of the later more scientific age, but they survived in the repertoire of many nineteenth-century fighters. The 'suit in chancery' meant grasping a man's head under one arm and punching him freely with the other fist. Dowling's book has, in its illustrations, a graphic print of this manoeuvre, which left the man in chancery in a helpless, humiliating, and of course highly vulnerable position. In 1821 Jack Randall beat Jack Martin in one round by the effective use of this tactic, pummelling Martin fiercely in the neck.

As for the cross-buttock* Dowling's description is both clear and vivid:

> When your sides come together you must manage to get your arm firmly over your adversary's neck, grasping his loose arm with the other hand—then shifting yourself to his front, get his crutch upon your hip or buttock, give him a cant over your shoulder—if well done his heels will go up in the air, he goes over with tremendous violence, and you fall upon his abdomen. The chances are that he is either insensible or is so shaken by the fall that he loses all power of resisting your future attacks.

* Grose's Dictionary (1785) listed 'cross-buttock' as a 'Particular lock or fall in the Broughtonian art, which Mr. Fielding observed, conveys more pleasurable sensations to the spectators than the patient'.

The whole point of technique is to win fights by defending oneself against attack and doling out the maximum punishment to one's own opponent. The targets of attack were first stated by Godfrey and then recapitulated by his successors with specious anatomical notes on the results of certain blows on the physique of the receiver. Godfrey listed the most hurtful blows as

> hitting under the Ear, between the Eye-brows, and about the stomach. I look upon the blow under the Ear to be as dangerous as any, if it alight between the Angle of the lower jaw to the neck. . . . The blows to the stomach are also very hurtful . . . the Vomitions produced by them I might account for, but I should run my anatomical impertinences too far.

In Mendoza's *Modern Art of Boxing*, published around 1792, the author lists the most telling blows as to

> the eye-brows, on the bridge of the nose, on the temple arteries, beneath the left ear, under the short ribs or in the kidneys, as it is termed, deprives the person struck of his breath, occasions an instant discharge of urine, puts him in the greatest torture and renders him for some time a cripple.

In the first volume of *Boxiana* many of the anatomical impertinences for which Godfrey apologised are repeated. This lengthy and unnecessary quasi-medical mumbo-jumbo was noted by Professor Wilson in *Blackwood's Magazine*. Alive as ever to the claims of specious learning, he praises the writer for his commendable seriousness . . . 'The scientific explanation would do credit to Astley Cooper* . . .'.

Bare fists wrought very considerable damage and the bare-knuckle fights of the prizering cannot be likened to modern boxing, when the contestants wear heavily padded gloves; and as we shall see, the rules under which the fights were fought were few in number and designed to protect the fighters from only the most obviously foul of blows. They were counselled to use the 'large knuckles of the hand . . . for they are rarely disabled . . .

---

* A famous surgeon at Guy's, whose lectures Keats attended when he joined the surgical practice at that hospital.

whereas the knuckles in the middle of the fingers frequently give way', and they were therefore advised to keep the fist tightly clenched.

The bare knuckle is penetrative in areas where the glove is comparatively innocuous; thus blows to the eyes, to the side of the neck or to the throat were particularly damaging. The constant appearance of 'claret' in descriptions of prizefighting is not mere graphics. There was invariably a lot of blood about, and it came not only from the nose but also from the mouth and the ears. It was stated as a matter of some surprise that 'scarcely any claret was spilt' when Ned Turner beat Jack Martin in 1819. One of the treatments favoured by the medical profession for restoring a badly punished fighter was to bleed him. After the loss of blood in the fight itself it is remarkable that the pugilists were able to survive a second dose of bloodletting on their systems. However, Jack Martin, beaten in one round by Randall, and Jack Power were two of many to receive this panacea. Casanova witnessed a prizefight at which one fighter seemed to be at the point of death. A surgeon was prepared to bleed him but was not permitted to do so because bets had by then been placed as to whether the man would recover or die!

The effects of bare-fist battles on the fighters was considerable and few of the fighters fought more than a dozen times in their careers. Certainly only a handful of the 'Receivers-General' were able to keep fighting and an analysis of the fights of the more successful pugilists shows that they rarely fought more than once or twice a year; nor did they remain long in competition. Jackson and Gully, the two most distinguished pugilists, each fought only three times in the prizering, as did Bob Gregson; and men like Jack Scroggins, Josh Hudson and Phil Sampson are remarkable in fighting more than a dozen times. The effects of bare-knuckle fighting on the combatants is seen most obviously in the number of fatalities in the ring. In the big matches there were surprisingly few deaths, but the provincial papers and the sporting magazines make frequent mention of ring deaths in minor battles.

Many fighters received injuries in the ring which led to permanent injury and in many cases to early death. Ben Brain beat Tom Johnson, but he was never able to defend the title, dying some months after his win of the injuries received in that fight, in which he had been frequently hit in the kidneys. In *Lavengro* Borrow says that his father nursed Brain for some months and that Ben died in his father's arms. There were many other pugilists who died early and whose deaths were said to be occasioned by overindulgence in drink—men like Dutch Sam, George Head, Molyneux, Jack Randall and Josh Hudson. Neither the word nor the concept 'punch-drunk' were current at the time and the danger of cumulative effects of hits to the head were not considered even by the detractors of boxing. It seems likely that many of the fighters suffered from some form of brain damage, and one thinks of such men as Jack Scroggins and Caleb Baldwin as likely subjects for this diagnosis.

The bare fist is itself subject to damage and there were several fighters who suffered from weak hands. The most famous was Tom Spring, who became Champion despite this handicap, which caused him to be given some most unflattering nicknames, like 'the Lady's Maid' and the 'Powder-Puff Fighter'. The elegant Tom Belcher had to retire from the prizering after his finger was broken when in contact with Dan Dogherty's ivories.

By no means all the fighters suffered permanent physical or mental damage from their contests. Jackson, Gully, Tom Belcher, Cribb, Spring, Jem Ward, Joe Ward and Langan, for example, all remained sharp and spry into a green old age.

The necessity of training was appreciated from the earliest days and the penalty of insufficient training was evidenced by Broughton's surprise defeat at the hands of Slack; and like the technique of fighting, the technique of training made rapid strides during our period. In Mendoza's *Modern Art of Boxing*, published when the Mendoza–Humphries rivalry was the talk of the town, we are informed that the following method of training can be recommended:

Your beverage at dinner should be wine and water and a glass or two of old hock afterwards; pass your afternoon in riding or walking, and about 8 o'clock you may eat for supper any light nourishing food; if opportunity serves use exercise again, such as throwing out the dumb-bells, etc. till you retire to rest. Be sure you take care to avoid excess either in food, wine or women.

Spend the morning in an early walk, of not more than a mile, first breaking your fast with a single gingerbread nut steeped (if not apt to inebriate) in Holland's. Return home slow to avoid heating the body and, in order to preserve it so lay cool at night.

On the morning of the fighting, eat only one slice of bread, well toasted, or a hard white biscuit toasted, and, if not too strong for the constitution, half a pint of good red wine, mulled with a tablespoon of brandy; this is to be taken an hour before the time of dressing. On the stage have your drink made of Holland's bitters, fine china orange juice, with some lump sugar to render it palatable.

Such a regimen must at least have ensured that the fighter went into battle in a relaxed frame of mind, if not in the best of physical condition. It was Captain Barclay, Cribb's patron, and himself a famed pedestrian, who first drew the attention of the boxing world to the inestimable value of good training. The second Cribb v Molyneux fight revealed the enormous advantage of a man in the peak of physical condition. Poor Molyneux was crushed.

When Barclay began to train him for this fight, Cribb weighed 16 stone (224lb) and 'from his mode of living in London and the confinement of a crowded city, he had become corpulent, big-bellied, full of gross humours and short-breathed'. Barclay took him up to Ury in the Highlands for 9 weeks. He was dosed with physic—and for the first two weeks he went walking and shooting. After this gentle start he began regular walking exercises, which at first amounted to 10–12 miles a day, soon after increased to 18–20; and he ran regularly, morning and evening, a quarter of a mile at the top of his speed. In the course of 5 weeks his weight was reduced to 14 stone 9lb (205lb). At this period he commenced his sweats and took three during the next 4 weeks.

His weight was reduced to 13 stone 5lb (187lb), which was considered to be his ideal fighting weight as he could not reduce further without weakening. During this time he sparred only occasionally.

Sir Harry Smith, commander of Wellington's Light Brigade at Vittoria in 1813, claimed that 'every man was in better wind than a trained pugilist'. The analogy might not have been used before Barclay's revolution. His training methods were clearly sounder than those which had been adopted before, but there are some details of his regimen which make fascinating reading. He was a great believer in the regular movement of the bowels: 'the persons trained should produce one stool per day; if that be *in form,* or shape, and of yellow tinge, he will have no occasion for physic'.

As for food and drink, 'veal and lamb should never be given, nor vegetables such as turnips, carrots or potatoes . . . as they are watery and difficult of digestion. Neither butter nor cheese is allowed . . . eggs are also forbidden, except the yolk taken raw in the morning'. Liquors must always be taken cold and 'home brewed beer, old but not bottled is the best', though 'the quantity should not exceed three pints a day'. Water should never be given and 'ardent spirits are strictly prohibited, however diluted'. And there was one more point. 'The *sexual intercourse* must vanish and be no more heard of, within the first week of training.'

Blackwood's Magazine made great sport with the detailed diets which were recommended for complete physical wellbeing. A parson of the Fancy contributed a paper on training which included the following diet:

> In the morning, at four of the clock, a serving-man doth enter my chamber, bringing me a cup containing half one quart of pig's urine, which I doe drink. . . . At breakfast I doe commonly eat 12 goose's eggs, dressed in whale's oil, wherefrom I experience much good effects. For dinner I doe chiefly prefer a roasted cat, whereof the hair has first been burned by the fire. If it be stuffed with salted herrings which are a good and pleasant fish, it will be

better. Cow's tripes with cabbage is likewise a dish which I much esteem. . . . I drink each two or three goblets of cordial spirit, whereof I prefer gin, as being of a diuretic nature, and salutiferous to the kidneys. My supper consisteth of a mess of potage, made with the fat of pork, and the whale's oil aforesaid; after which I do drink another cup of pig's urine, which helpeth digestion and maketh me to sleep sound.

Parodies apart, there seems no doubt that many of the diets recommended to athletes suffered from the judgement that what was pleasing to the palate was well suited to the stomach.

There was no doubt that Cribb thrived on Barclay's regimen, as did Barclay himself. But there were men, as there always have been, who found the strict demands of training too much for their temperaments. Such a man was Donnelly. 'Dan's opinion was so strongly grounded that excess of any kind would not hurt him, that he acted as he pleased.' And he was addicted to two of the things which Captain Barclay forbade in training—women and drink. During training he would steal out after dark to seek his 'game', and indeed after his battle with Oliver 'it was not only found out, but he acknowledged that he had contracted a disease in the promiscuousness of his amours'. As for the ardent spirits which Barclay had forbidden, poor Dan would take 'a drop of the stuff with him to bed to prevent his lying awake'.

One of the favoured training camps was Wheeler's house at Riddlesdown, three or four miles from Croydon. Wheeler recorded that of thirty men who had trained there twenty-four had won. One of the twenty-four was Donnelly, who did not find the four miles to Croydon too far to go in search of his favourite game. There was a steep hill in front of Wheeler's house which was considered useful in building up stamina, a fighter having to run up it as a regular feature of his training. It is interesting to note that Neat had the ignominy of breaking his arm while making such a training run before his engagement with Tom Spring. Jem Ward trained for his fight with Josh Hudson by climbing the Hampstead Hills, which had always been the favourite training ground for the unbeaten Jack Randall. Josh Hudson, when he chose to train, preferred to take his dogs coursing. He claimed to have lost twenty pounds in weight for one fight by following the dogs for five hours at a stretch.

Some fighters, like Hall of Birmingham, were always in training and many of the lesser men got their training on the job. Not for many the fast coach and pair provided by the patron; when West-country Dick fought Street in 1817 Dick had been 'navigating' early in the morning, and 'padded the hoof to Hale'. His opponent Street walked twenty-two miles to the fight. The London-based favourites, however, had to get away from the fleshpots of the sporting houses and the attention of the Fancy when they needed to prepare for a fight. But many could not drag themselves away. Dutch Sam claimed to train on three glasses of gin taken three times a day and Josh Hudson, after taking over the Half Moon Tap, appeared in the ring like 'Two Single Gentlemen rolled into ONE'.

The trainer was clearly an important character, as we have seen from the success of Captain Barclay. He remained close to the fighter at a time when that man was often undergoing an unpleasantly spartan regimen and the lack of convivial company. A strong-minded yet sympathetic trainer was, therefore, of the utmost value in insisting on the regularity of the training and at the same time providing sympathetic and entertaining companionship. The 'Trainer's Rondo' by 'Bernard Breakwindow' illustrates the bluff insistence on a regular discipline which the trainer must urge on his fighter:

> Up in the morning, near the pump-handle,
> There I stand, Jack, with a heart full of glee;
> Come, open each peeper,
> You featherbed sleeper,
> And up in the morning, Jack Randall, with me.
> Tho' in the Fives Court, you can fib it and spar it,
> And prove of neat hits both a giver and taker;
> Yet 'tis morn's early rising, and beef steaks, and claret,
> Will string up your nerves and wap Martin the Baker.

The implicit trust which a fighter should have in his trainer was not demonstrated on one occasion, when Bill Neat 'openly and distinctly accused his trainer of unfair dealings towards him with having laid his bets against his winning his fight against Hickman'.

Not much equipment was used in training compared with the training aids of a modern gymnasium. Dumb-bells, however, came into regular use in the nineteenth century. Ned Turner, with the kind of unsolicited testimonial with which we are now familiar, told Pierce Egan that when he first began to use dumb-bells he could scarcely count fifteen before feeling tired; but after a little practice and perseverance he was able to pass them backwards and forwards upwards of 300 times. Massage was coming into use late in our period, when Bee recommended 'that species of rubbing with the hand or friction', which 'has been found a highly serviceable kind of treatment in all cases of rheumatic afflictions or pains in the limbs'.

The gymnasia that were widely famed belonged to the ex-boxers with the reputation of being good teachers. Broughton had taught sparring at his amphitheatre, but the first of the modern masters to teach was Mendoza, who opened the Old Lyceum Theatre in the Strand as a school for sparring. His lessons were expensive and 'he knocked the heads of the noble lords and right honourables about with as much indifference as if they had been barber's blocks, in order to beat instructions into their pericraniums'. Mendoza also toured the country giving lessons.

Bill Richmond was another successful teacher, and his son, Young Richmond, taught the rudiments of the art to Prince George of Cambridge. George Head was undoubtedly one of the best teachers of his day and he brought out more promising millers than any of the other teachers, his pupils including Shock Jem, Ned Painter, Parish the Waterman, Tom Spring, Jack Martin and Jack Power.

The two most remarkable teachers, however, were men who taught the art of self-defence to the amateurs rather than to potential prizefighters. They were Gentleman John Jackson, and William Fuller, who was designated 'the Jackson of America' and in his way was as remarkable a character as Jackson himself. Fuller had fought in the prizering and indeed had fought a draw with Molyneux. The first notice we have of him, in the early part of his career, tells us that 'he may attain eminence if he does not creep too much into favour with himself'. In 1818 he became clerk of the racecourse at Valenciennes, where he opened a subscription room for instruction in the art of self-defence. He is said to have induced many Frenchmen to have a trial à l'Anglaise. He moved from France to America and opened a gymnasium in Chicago, where he appeared as Gentleman Jackson in a production of Tom and Jerry at the Charleston Theatre. Clearly he was an enterprising man and his manners and abilities made him a fortune. The last glimpse we have of him is from New York where he was living as a retired gentleman.

Fuller's model was John Jackson, who, for twenty years before Fuller set up as a teacher, had ruled the world of pugilism from his rooms at 13 Bond Street. Byron took his lessons from him and described him, at various times, as 'my corporeal pastor and master', 'Professor of Pugilism', and the 'Emperor of Pugilism'. Jackson was more widely known as the 'Commander-in-Chief' of the prizering. His subscription list included many distinguished men and his rooms were open three times a week during the season. It was here that 'everything respecting the prize-ring and connected with pugilism are determined'.

Vincent Dowling, the editor of Bell's Life, knew Jackson well and his description in Fistiana of Jackson's Rooms and his teaching methods give an excellent picture.

> Here all the élite of the fashionable world were daily assembled; noblemen and gentlemen of the highest rank did not disdain to take the gloves with the accomplished Jackson and the 'set's-to' even amongst themselves evinced a knowledge of the science, a power of endurance, and a vigour equal, if not in many instances superior, to the public pugilists of the time, with whom they

OPPOSITE   *Mendoza (James Gillray)*

DUNN. WARD. FUTRELL. JACKSON. JOHNSON. WYNDHAM. SMITH. HUMPH

ART OF SELF DEFENCE. Tom and Jerry receiving Instruction from Mr Jackson

often tried their hands and came off victorious; qualities, the value of which, in after life, they acknowledged when the roar of battle, or the death struggle with the foes of their country, by land or sea, required the exercise of those energies which the preparative practice of Jackson's Room had nurtured and developed. In these associations there was none of the finnikin foppery of modern times; there were no apprehensions of the derangement of well-curled locks or pretty faces; men, and noblemen too, met foot to foot and fist to fist, regardless of consequence, dealing such blows at each other's heads as often deprived them of momentary sensation.

Mr. Jackson's mode of instruction was at once philosophical and practical. Himself the most accomplished boxer of his day he knew the principles upon which attack or defence were to be conducted; and these he explained, not by showing results, but by demonstrating 'cause and effect' with a master mind and a master hand. He taught his pupils to feel that personal confidence and the contempt of danger were the first and best qualities of a pugilist. He showed them, that to hit with effect, they must first judge their distance, that is to say, to judge when the delivery of a blow would produce the most conclusive consequence; for, as he properly inculated, if a blow reached its destination short of weight and vigour of muscle by which it ought to be propelled, like a spent shot it was of little avail, and had better not be attempted. He showed that men ought to fight as well with their legs as with their hands; and that unless they were quick and active with the former, so as to spring in and out as opportunity demanded, the intent of the latter would be altogether frustrated. He decried all stiffness of position, and showed that the impulses of nature were always best aided by that light, springing ease, which in the ordinary movements of man, when uninfluenced by the posture master, were obvious and inherent. He showed that with the body a little bent, the head and shoulders forward, and the knees in like manner elastic and easy, and with the hands well up, a man was prepared for advance or retreat, as the quickness of his eye and the exercise of his self-possession might suggest.

Ambidexterity, that is the power of hitting and stopping with the left and right with equal quickness, he also strongly inculcated, and, by his own example, showed that he could stop the 'one, two' (hits with both hands) either with his right or left hand, and either return with the same hand, or bring in the reserve with

I

stunning force. He clearly showed that fighting for the body was a dangerous game; for, with a well-instructed pugilist, he who attempted it was sure to be met in the head before his knuckles reached the body of his antagonist, and with double force too, because he gave the impetus of his own rush to the coming blow. The lessons were conveyed in such a way as to produce conviction; for, as Mr. Jackson defied any man to hit him, he always called upon his pupil to try his own tactics, and the issue invariably verified the truth of his axiom, whatever it might be.

In 1822 the *Fancy Gazette* recorded that Mr Jackson's services to the ring 'have long lain the Amateurs under obligations which their subscriptions to his milling rooms do but faintly discharge. They have felt this some time; and a splendid service of plate is now preparing for him at Messrs Clark, Cheapside'. The plate which was presented later that year was worth over £300.

The closing of Jackson's Rooms in 1824 brought to an end the close association of the amateurs with the sport and 'the link that bound the highest patrons of the Fancy together might be said to be at an end'.

CHAPTER EIGHT

The Fives Court and the Benefits

Run, dandies, run, all London now are milling it;
All to the Fives Court the match to view are gone.
BERNARD BREAKWINDOW: *Jack Randall's Diary*

It is usual for ritual acts to have a place sacred to their mysteries and the temple dedicated to the performance of pugilism was the Fives Court. From 1802 until it was pulled down to enable the site to be redeveloped in 1826, the Fives Court in Little St Martin's Street, London, was the showplace of pugilism. It was here that benefits were held for the fighters, and occasionally for other causes, and it was here that the fighters had the opportunity of showing off their points and perfections in the fistic art. Aspiring pugilists were able to demonstrate their claim to

137

patronage or to fight for a Pugilistic Club purse. Here challenges were given, stakes put down, and matches made. In Egan's words the Fives Court also represented 'an animated inspiring lounge for the nobility and heavy swells, and to which might be added an attraction in general to the public'.

There had been sparring exhibitions before Mendoza and Bill Warr appeared at the Fives Court in 1802. Mendoza and Warr had taught sparring at Capelcourt and at the Lyceum Theatre in the Strand and they had been engaged by the proprietors of the Theatre Royal, Covent Garden, to exhibit their tactics as a new form of theatrical attraction. But their appearance at the Fives Court instituted a new tradition of benefits for which tickets were issued in advance and attendance publicly solicited by means of handbills and posters.

The Court was a large oblong structure with high walls, 'the light being admitted through interstices at the top, covered with net work to prevent the loss of balls in Fives or tennis', for which the Court was still used on weekdays. For some years after 1802 the bouts were held on the floor of the Court and it was not until some years later that a 4ft stage was erected, at the suggestion of the negro Bill Richmond and adopted by Tom Cribb. The stage was temporary and was dismantled after the fight so that the Court could revert to its original purpose.

Richmond, whose public house the Horse and Dolphin was conveniently sited next door to the Court, was the first to spar without a vest or shirt, in order that the spectators might admire the muscular development of the fighters and 'provide a study for the sculptor'. Benjamin Haydon, the artist, was a visitor and Joseph Farington, the President of the Royal Academy, attended an exhibition at the Fives Court in 1808 and enquired of Dutch Sam and John Gully their heights and weights. He recorded that John Rossi, the sculptor, 'much admired Dutch Sam's figure on account of the *symmetry* and the *parts being expressed*'.

When the first exhibitions were given at the Court the price of admission varied from two *bobs* (2s) or *half-a-bull* (2s 6d) up to three *bobs* and a *bender* (3s 6d), but it soon became standardised at 3s. The only exception to this was a small elevated dressing-room at one end, with a window looking into the Court, set apart, Dowling tells us, for the aristocracy; 'here was often seen congregated some dozens of noblemen and persons of high rank, whose liberal contributions (many of them giving a guinea for a ticket) added greatly to the receipts of the beneficiary'.

Tickets were sold in the various sporting houses, particularly in Richmond's house and the Castle Tavern, in the week before the benefit, and the beneficiary himself would tout the tickets about the town. In *Real Life in London* Bitton, the Jew, after entertaining the customers of a sporting house with card tricks and a chaunt, is recorded as approaching Tom and Bob with some cards in his hand. At first they thought that he was going to perform some further tricks but he presented them with a card that 'announced his benefit for the next week at the Fives Court, when all the *prime lads* of the *ring* had promised to exhibit . . . each of the party being supplied with a ticket, Bitton canvassed the room for other customers'. On the day of the benefit the beneficiary stood at the entrance himself 'with a capacious money-box' to collect the entrance money from those who had not previously bought tickets and to solicit further contributions.

The Court held up to 1,000 spectators and if the beneficiary were a current favourite, or if he had succeeded in persuading some current stars to appear, the Court could be filled and the proceeds approach £200. The charge to the beneficiary for the hire of the Court was £8 and he had further expenses for printing and distributing the posters and handbills, paying the master of ceremonies and satisfying the demands of the minor coves who exhibited in the early bouts. No pugilist could obtain the Fives Court for his benefit without the acquiescence and patronage of John Jackson. The influence of Jackson 'gave him possession of the key which was to open the pockets of the amateurs and the public' to deserving pugilists. Jackson, being the man he was, there were few grievances, though one or two, including Joe

Norton, Deaf Davis and Harry Harmer, 'made complaints in a corner that they had been overlooked'; and in the spring of 1821 Jackson refused to allow an application from his old rival Mendoza to use the Court, his unrelenting dislike of the Jew being the one blind spot in an otherwise generous character.

The master of ceremonies at the Fives Court was for long old Joe Norton, who was paid 8s 6d per diem for these services. Joe, who acted as a second in many prizefights, was 'a very useful and intelligent person'. He introduced the boxers to the audience and he prepared the boxers' gloves and equipment. 'Joe is also very civil, obliging and communicative to the persons that attend the Fives Court and who may be anxious to obtain information respecting the merits of the pugilists.' As Jackson would not permit him the use of the Court for his own benefits, he used to take his benefits at a tavern. Poor Joe died in Harry Harmer's tavern a day or two after being assaulted by Hickman, the 'Gasman', who lost his temper with the old man. As master of ceremonies Norton was assisted by Lennox and after his death in 1822 Tom 'Paddington' Jones took over his role.

The bouts, which were always glove fights as opposed to the bare fists of the prizering, commenced with the third-raters, occasionally with novices, and succeeding matches were in the scale of merit of the boxers, the proceedings ending with a 'wind-up' between the beneficiary and his selected opponent. The novices were not paid but were usually showered with copper 'often agreeably relieved by the lights and shades of silver'.

More usually, however, the opening bouts featured the regular minor coves, like Lennox, Mason, Gidgeon and Gadzee, who received a remuneration for their services from the fighter for whose benefit they were exhibiting. Lennox, 'the Colonel', was considered the prologue to any performance and his battles with Mason and later with Little Gadzee formed an exhilarating opening to the proceedings, the little men buzzing about the ring displaying great vigour and speed. In fact their style was probably much more like modern boxing than much of what was to follow. But constant battles between the same two men became constantly more stylised, not to say tedious. *Bell's Life*, reporting on a benefit in 1825, by which time Lennox was aged 50, said:

> Lennox and Gadzee . . . have worn themselves and the patience of spectators thin by the repetition of their appearance . . . as usual they performed an overture upon each other's noses, and met with applause in proportion to the degree of punishment which they received and gave.

After the regulars the first-raters would appear, performing unpaid for the benefit of a colleague. The beneficiary would naturally try to secure the services of those fighters in the news, whose names he would publish in his handbills. It was not unknown for beneficiaries deliberately to advertise the appearance of particular stars, while having no guarantee that they would appear. Harry Harmer, taking a benefit in March 1822, advertised that Bill Neat would take part, Neat being the current hero from his defeat of the 'Gasman'. However, Neat did not appear, nor did George Head, advertised as the prime attraction for Joe Parish's benefit the following month. By 1825 this practice was common.

There were some fighters who were always ready to exhibit for their colleagues' benefit, and others who were less enthusiastic. Isaac Bitton was always ready to strip and do his best at the Fives Court, and when, at one of his own benefits, there were few pugilists of note exhibiting *Bell's Life* declared it 'a circumstance which does not redound much to the liberality of their spirit'.

The most elegant of all the sparrers remained Tom Belcher, who at 5ft 9in and under 11 stone (154lb), demonstrated his skills against the bigger men at the Fives Court until the age of 40. At Cribb's benefit in 1814 Belcher gave a brilliant exhibition of skilful boxing against the Champion himself, a man 3 stone heavier. Another popular man with the gloves was Bill Richmond, whose skill in moving away from an opponent was greatly admired. There were complaints from time to time of conditions at the

Fives Court. Despite the raised stage it was said that it was not easy for those at the back to see the boxers when the Court was crowded, as it frequently was. Bee suggested that this evil could be overcome by laying down 2in deal planks all round the Court against the walls so that the 'multum in parvo' men would be enabled to look over the shoulders of those blessed with greater length of limb.

The Court could also get cold for the spectator in the late winter. At the benefit for Tom Hickman's widow, held on 5 February 1823, 'the weather was extremely cold, the Court damp by its constant exposure to the action of the atmosphere, and the company felt the effects of both'. The complainant ends with the heartfelt plea: 'Let no pugilist proclaim another meeting this spring without the precaution of covering the floor with a sawyer's carpet'.

Apart from the complaints of a poor view from the back of the Court and rising damp, there was a third complaint about conditions in the Court: this was the danger from pickpockets and other ruffians. The Fives Court was open to everybody, so long, says Egan, 'as the tip for admission was settled'. This being so it was a fine place for characters of all sorts—of all sizes—of all grades; and in this democratic atmosphere gentlemen visiting the Court jostled with the lower orders and with prigs and pickpockets. Bee declared:

> it sometimes degenerates into a struggle between the fingers of one part of the spectators and the pockets of the other part, the former of whom line the dark passage and form strings of depredations in the streets adjoining, through which it is frequently dangerous to pass.

But there were criticisms of an even more serious nature, matters of principle which were to bring an end to these exhibitions altogether. The bouts at the Fives Court were not matches, they were exhibition bouts of sparring, a representation of the prizering battle but not the real thing. Some thought the exercise of sparring positively dangerous to a pugilist as inducing in him reactions which would be disastrous in the prizering in a bare-fist battle. This school of thought is summed up in the couplet:

A little sparring is a dangerous thing,
Drink deep or taste not of the *milling* RING.

But there is no doubt that many of the pugilists improved their techniques by exhibiting with the masters like Tom Belcher at the Fives Court and there is no evidence that sparring took away 'from the natural powers of manhood'. Most informed opinion reflected that of Egan in 1818: 'There may be a great difference between sparring and fighting; one may be very courageous in play, whose heart would be intimidated in real action . . . but cowardice is not produced in sparring'.

In 1821 there was a further complaint, which was of greater significance. Egan, again, records: 'The real judges and grandees of the prizering assert that it (the sparring benefit) prevents actual combats, while the glove market affords such plentiful harvest'. The Fives Court, while being a most useful supplement to the prizering, was no real substitute, and it depended for its popularity on the vigour of the sport itself. By providing fighters with financial rewards without the regular necessity of real combat in the prizering it ultimately proved to be of disservice to the sport. In 1821 Egan said that the Pugilistic Club intended to regulate this matter, but in fact it never did.

Three years earlier, in 1818, Egan had noted that there were a good many benefits at the Fives Court and in 1821:

the benefits have of late become so numerous that the amateurs complain that they can scarcely get three *whiffs* out of their *steamer*, or cool their *chaffers* with a *heavy wet*, than their *ogles* are made to *wink* at the sight of a benefit ticket, and, to prevent being thought *scaly* three *bobs* are punished beyond redemption.

Benefits had proved so popular with the pugilists that they had come in danger of being overplayed. In 1822 Bee complained of the numerous appeals on the pocket which 'disgust alike the generous and seedy part of the pugilistic public'.

This circumstance had in part come about by the opening of the Royal Tennis Court in Great Windmill St, Haymarket, to sparring exhibitions. The first benefit at the Tennis Court was on behalf of Bill Richmond and was held on 20 February 1820. The proprietor of the Tennis Court, Mr Hunt, started a series of sparring exhibitions for his own benefit and he retained a number of the lesser fighters, charging 1s a head for entrance. He was successful in attracting the public and engaged one or two good fighters, including Peter Crawley, Abraham Belasco and the negro Kendrick, whom he paid between £2 and £3 a week. But the pugilists in general saw the Tennis Court as taking away the 'cheese-parings and candle-ends of their hard earned profession', and it was soon denominated the 'opposition place'.

Jack Scroggins had issued tickets for a benefit to be held in the Tennis Court before this blow-up occurred and he immediately announced that the benefit would be held in the Fives Court, as there alone 'the first rate pugilists would exhibit'. Among other squibs and efforts at lawsuits to thwart each other, the following duet was issued:

TENNIS COURT
Since Bruisers stick up for their rights
It's time for me to be *leary*,
So their patrons I'll treat to sham fights,
Till damme, I'll make 'em quite queery.

FIVES COURT
Pooh, nonsense, your threats I'll defy,
Altho' I'm not such a swell
As to looks, why that's all my eye,
While I suit the Fancy as well.

TENNIS COURT
It isn't the Fancy I want,
But the blunt from their pockets to draw,
I've two sides where I customers plant,
A thing you ne'er before saw.

FIVES COURT
The swells I shall treat with respect,
To my friends I'll always be civil,
But if ever I gammon select
May I be floored by the Devil.

TENNIS COURT
The Public approve of my plan
'T has met with unbounded applause;
So I'll hum 'em as long as I can,
In spite of all honour and laws.

FIVES COURT
Who cares for your airs and your graces
Not I—you may think it is strange
For I'm down to your cues and your maces,
And know something about the *Exchange*.

TENNIS COURT
A fig for your chaffing and slum,
So that flats I can find pretty plenty,
Your threats are all a mere hum,
Where you have a quid I have twenty.

FIVES COURT
Damn that fellow, I say to your face,
Who has plenty of blunt in his cly,
Who'd push an honest man out of his place,
Or to take from him his living would try.

The Tennis Court was certainly not easily disregarded and with the stage that Ben Burns had provided, it was as well equipped as the Fives Court. The rivalry between the two was to end in 1826 when the Fives Court was demolished, the last benefit held there being Peter Warren's on 30 August 1825. The Tennis Court was left as the sole arena for benefits and exhibitions except for occasional bouts in a theatre or public house. But as the reputation of pugilism fell into decline in the late 1820s, patronage was withdrawn and when the benefits ceased to be profitable the proprietor let the Court for another purpose and the pugilists lost their showplace. To some extent, the pugilists themselves had killed the goose that laid the golden egg, for they had abused their privileges by organising too many benefits and by announcing (in their posters and handbills) men who never appeared. The loss of a showplace was part cause and part effect of the general malaise that settled on pugilism in the years following Jackson's retirement. For twenty-five years the Fives Court had had a profound influence on the sport. It had helped to make it more respectable, with gentlemen attending who would not think of going to a prizefight. It had introduced new fighters to the Fancy and, perhaps most important of all, the exhibitions had educated both the fighters and the spectators in the finer points of the sweet science. Many of the rough diamonds of the ring, men like Tom Shelton and Josh Hudson, were greatly improved by their sparring with the gloves and it is from the science displayed and nourished in the Courts that modern boxing has developed.

There are several excellent prints of the Fives Court. That by Blake, engraved by Turner, is perhaps the best, though containing certain anachronisms and showing the spectators facing the painter with their backs to the bout between Randall and Martin. Despite its faults, however, it is a notable picture of the Court in its palmy days. A later picture by Robert Cruikshank, dated 1822, is of almost equal interest (p 151). It is not the romantic conception of Blake and reflects perhaps the diminishing excitement of the exhibitions in the later history of the Court.

CHAPTER NINE

The Fancy

Ever let the fancy roam,
Pleasure never is at home.

JOHN KEATS: *Fancy*

'How truly English that particular species which has received the dignity of the definite article—"THE FANCY",' wrote Jon Bee in the *Fancy Gazette* for February 1822. But as with many English institutions it is difficult to capture the full meaning in a definition. Reynolds came closest with the words 'Life preserved in Spirit', but it is a definition for connoisseurs and the cognoscenti rather than the common man.

The Fancy is usually understood as the followers of boxing, the fighters, the patrons, the trainers, the crowds and all those whose fancy was the prizering. It is roughly correct to define the Fancy thus and it is with the world of boxing that this chapter will be mainly concerned. But as the Fancy is as much inspiration as actuality it deserves a word or two of amplification.

On the first page of the first volume of *Boxiana* Egan suggests that 'the Fancy simply means any person who is fond of a particular amusement or closely attached to some subject'. The high priest and chronicler of the Fancy did not restrict the term to the followers of boxing, but allowed that it comprehended all sporting characters with a particular enthusiasm. Reynolds, writing in 1820, gives what is probably the best of all definitions, though not entirely comprehensive:

> *Fancy*'s a term for every blackguardism—
> A term for favourite men and favourite cocks—
> A term for gentlemen who make a schism
> Without the lobby or within the box—
> For the best rogues of polish'd vulgarism,
> And those who deal in scientific knocks—
> For bull-dog breeders, badger-baiters—all
> Who live in gin and jail, or not at all.

Reynolds makes clear that a definition of the Fancy cannot be confined to the followers of boxing, but comprehends the followers of the other fancy sports, cockfighting, dogfighting, and bear and badger baiting. More than this, it is not restricted to sport as such. Corinthian Tom was one of the Fancy and his singleminded pursuit was pleasure. Most enthusiasts are singleminded to a certain degree and the dedicated pursuit of their own interests necessarily made the Fancy ignore many other considerations.

When Hazlitt accused the Fancy of having no imagination, of judging what has been rather than what is to be, he was only partly right. The Fancy, as Hazlitt himself said, is the 'most practical of all things', as befits one who puts his money to the touch, and yet there are 'as many feuds, factions, prejudices and pedantic notions in the Fancy as in the state or in the schools'. The Fancy consists of two elements, the practical and the optimistic, and within the area of its interest the Fancy is a slave to its passions, relying as much on imagination and conjecture as matters of fact. There can be few more imaginative than those who imagine that their man, or their cock, can beat the Champion, and are prepared to put their money to the trial.

Hazlitt was certainly right, however, to suggest that many members of the Fancy were restricted in their topics of conversation.

My friend the Trainer was confined in his topics to fighting dogs and men, to bears and badgers; beyond this he was quite chapfallen, had not a word to throw at a dog, and very wisely fell asleep when any other game was started.

Like all enthusiasts, the member of the Fancy required an enthusiastic audience and he usually took care to move in areas where such a response would be guaranteed, at the ringside or in the sporting houses or Tattersall's Rooms. The Fancy could indeed be a shocking bore. Even 'Paul Pry' admitted there was a good deal of *routine* about their conversation,

> and they scarcely ever open their mouths without finishing the sentences with 'I'll bet you 2 to 1, or 6 to 4 . . .'. Without a bet amongst this sort of gentry, anything like interest seems to evaporate from their minds, and the whole of their arguments become little else than stale, flat and unprofitable.

'Jonathan Kentucky', writing in the literary magazine, *The New Monthly*, said that the Fancy form 'a distinct class among the innumerable sects into which England is divided. They are by no means confined to the lower orders, but may reckon a large proportion of rank and talent among their numbers'. In an age devoted to the doctrine of exclusivity the Fancy was a democratic or, perhaps better, a polyglot group, united only in their devotion to their own fancy. But when the Fancy assembled at a fight, or in Tattersall's settling rooms, all men were equal. The Duke of Clarence, later William IV, is said to have been at a fight at Moulsey Hurst when he saw a nobleman looking with distaste at the crowds. The Duke addressed him: 'Be pleased to recollect, my lord, that we are all Englishmen here; and as for places we must do the best we can for ourselves'. We need not doubt that the anecdote is apocryphal, but it contains an essential truth.

Around a prizering or a cockpit, 'every greasy hero or sooty chief placed himself by the side of the swells without any apology as feeling he had the right to do so'. Egan said: 'Selection is entirely out of the question . . . the noble lord and the needy commoner, are both at home after they have paid their tip for admission'. When they visited Tattersall's Rooms Corinthian Tom told Jerry in *Life in London*: 'The best judge of sporting events is the best man here. The Duke and the Parliamentary Orator, if they do not know the properties of a horse are little more than cyphers'.

Jerry, when he visited the Royal Cockpit at Tufton Street, noted with surprise the

> flue-fakers [chimney-sweeps], dustmen, lamp-lighters, stage-coachmen, bakers, farmers, barristers, swells, butchers, dog-fanciers, grooms, donkey-boys, weavers, snobs, market-men, watermen, honourables, sprigs of the nobility, M.P.'s, mail-guards, swaddies, etc., all in one rude contact, jostling and pushing against each other, when the doors were opened to procure a front seat.

The Corinthian explained to his country-cousin, Jerry:

> They are all sporting characters and are all touched more or less with the scene before them; and the flue-faker will drop his *bender* [sixpence] with as much pluck as the Honourable does his *fifty*, to support his opinion. The *spirit* is quite the same and it is only the *blunt* [money] that makes the difference.

Egan, who was a far more subtle observer of the social scene than he has been given credit for, noted one unusual point about an assembly of the Fancy. 'There is no intimacy or association about it. A man may be well-known here; he may also in his turn know everybody . . . yet be quite a stranger to their habits and connexions with society.' The negro Richmond understood these same nuances. We are told that 'in the temporary elevation of the moment, he still recollects that [though] the CORINTHIAN FANCIER may closely connect himself with *milling*, there are times when he has a different character to support, and must not be intruded upon'.

In the last analysis the Fancy belonged to the lower orders, for they were the permanent residents of Fancy's edifice, and the swells remained the visitors, however much at home they found themselves.

OPPOSITE   above *The Daffy Club from 'The English Spy'* (*Robert Cruikshank*); below *The Fives Court from 'The Annals of Sporting and Fancy Gazette'* (*Robert Cruikshank*)

ELECTION OF THE FANCY.

Cy. DAVIS,

Respectfully solicits the VOTES and INTERESTS of the AMATEURS at the

ROYAL TENNIS COURT,

Great Windmill Street, Haymarket,

On THURSDAY, MARCH 16, 1820,

BEING THE DAY FIXED FOR HIS ELECTION,

NEAT AND CABBAGE,
TWO CANDIDATES

From Bristol, also offer their Services to the Public on this Occasion, and

A WARM CONTEST IS EXPECTED,

In consequence of those well known Metropolitan Heroes of the Ring, *Messrs. Cribb, Belcher, Harmer, Oliver, Randall, Richmond, Eales, Turner, Martin, Reynolds, Sutton, &c.* being likewise determined to put in their Claims for the attention of the Sporting World.

The Polling will commence at Two o'Clock, and PLUMPERS will be the Order of the Day.

The TALENTS of the various Candidates are of the most STRIKING description; their ARGUMENTS will be perfectly demonstrative; the advantages of a good CONSTITUTION clearly shown; and the essential services portrayed, in DEFENDING it from all Attacks.

The State of the POLL will be declared at 5 o'Clock.

The access to the Hustings will be rendered pleasant and easy to the Voters; and QUALIFICATION TICKETS, at Three Shillings each, to be had at the Bar.

If the 'best judge respecting sporting events' was acknowledged
to be the best man there then the best man was undoubtedly
Bill Gibbons. Bill was the completest Fancier in the circle, being
knowledgeable on those sports dear to the heart of the Fancy—
milling, dogfighting and baiting. He was born in the borough of
St Giles on 28 September 1757, and 'cut his stick' at Lambeth,
London, in December 1827, his demise proving a deathblow to
the Fancy.

Gibbons was a coach wheelwright by trade, but a 'loose fish'
by calling:

> In all sports of the Fancy see Bill take the lead—
> When hunting the badger or bull of true breed
> With rum trotting neddies for speed or 'Gainst time,
> And tykes that will mill with the primest of prime.
> To fight or to second, to Bill 'tis the same—
> And a cove that is flash to the CHANCE of the game.
> In the ring truly useful—full of spunk at a hunt
> And a BOXER that knows the true value of blunt;
> Tho' quite partial to milling, yet averse to all strife,
> Yet down to the tricks and will live all his LIFE.

Above all Bill was noted as the 'Commissary-General' of the
prizering, being entrusted by the Pugilistic Club with the ropes
and stakes. These he took to all fights, races or other meetings
where fights might be anticipated for a purse or stake. For these
services he was paid 2 guineas a day from the Club's fund,
which John Jackson dispensed. The role of ringmaker was of
particular importance for, as we have seen, the venue of a prizefight could not be announced in advance for fear of magisterial
interference. It became necessary to ascertain the venue of a fight
by word of mouth or, even better, by following Bill Gibbons.

> Bill Gibbons, who was well known on the road, and was speeding
> down pretty sharp, was followed by crowds of vehicles of all
> descriptions; as many to whom the place of meeting was but
> conjectured, upon seeing him, felt assured of being on the right
> track.

K

POSITE *A handbill advertising a benefit at the Fives Court*

It was said that those who bet on the same side as Bill Gibbons were seldom on the wrong scent, but this was as much because of his expert knowledge as because of dishonesty. Pierce Egan, however, told one or two interesting tales after Bill's death. Gibbons had supplied spaniels and other fancy animals to the wives of some of his clients and being an 'insinnivating' sort of fellow, 'extremely humble in his deportment and mildness itself when addressing the above high-born dames, he used to sell them valuable shawls, French laces, veils, etc. Gibbons told the ladies he had the *knack* of getting them into his possession, but the Excise officers called it "smuggling" and on one memorable occasion they insisted they were in the right. The Commissioners also backed their opinion, and very politely informed Mr Gibbons that he must pay into the Court £200 for his error'.

Bill was always accompanied by his dog, his 'partner' as he called him. Indeed Sir Walter Scott told Thomas Hood that he did not care to have his animals with him in London, for fear he should be taken for Bill Gibbons. Bill was truly an 'asterisk to the Fancy', his bulky form and his dog being the signposts to the mill, the Fives Court or the bait: 'with his slouched hat, his hardy muzzle, that rivals the beauty of one of his own bull-dogs,—his fore-*grinders* [teeth] sticking out of his *gob* [mouth] like *chevaux de frise* and his *mauleys* [hands] in the pockets of his *upper benjamin* [overcoat]'. He was an original, the Fancy made flesh, and 'one who reduced the game of chance to a CERTAINTY'. His only oath, oft repeated, itself became a catchphrase of the Fancy, and 'Burn my breeches', were said to be the last words of one who was rightly termed the 'pendulum that kept the sporting world in motion'.

The Fancy was seen in its collective strength when travelling on the road to a fight:

Here were to be seen the NIB SPRIGS in their gigs, buggies and *dog carts*—and the TIDY ONES on their *trotters*, all alive and leaping. The *bang-up blades* were pushing their *prads* [horses] along in gay style, accompanied by two friends, that is to say, a *biped* and a *quadruped.* The *queer fancy lads,* who had hired hacks from the livery stable keepers, were kicking up a dust, and here and there rolling from their *prancers,* in their native soil; while the *neck or nothing boys,* with no prospect but a WHEREAS [bailiff's writ] before their eyes, were as heedless of their personal safety as they were of their Creditor's property. Jaded hacks and crazy vehicles were to be seen on all sides—here lay a *bank-rupt* cart with the panels *knock'd in,* and its driver with an eye *knock'd out,* the horse lamed, and the concern completely *knocked up,* just before the Auctioneer was called in, and his effects *knocked down.* There was another of the same description, with a harum-scarum devil of a half-breed, making his way at all risks, at a full gallop, as unmanageable in his career as his driver had been in his speculations; dust flying, women sprawling, men bawling, dogs barking, and the multitude continually increasing. *Scants, Scamps, Lords, Loungers, and Lacqueys—Costermongers from Tothill Fields* —and the Bloods from Bermondsey, completely lined the road as far as the eye could reach.

On the day of a fight then the road would be filled with the Fancy on a variety of horses, in a variety of vehicles or 'padding the hoof' amid scenes of the greatest excitement and confusion. More often than not the fight was at Moulsey Hurst and for a description of the experience of individual members of the Fancy on the road to Moulsey I look to two poems.

That by Reynolds describes a gentleman's progress and the second, from a crambonian chaunt in Egan's *Book of Sports,* describes the progress of the rag, tag and bobtail fanciers. (Students of parody, or plagiarism, may wish to compare *Don Juan,* Canto I, verses CXXII et seq with the Reynolds' poem.)

First, the gentleman:

> 'Tis Life to see the first day stain
> With sallow light the window pane
> . . . .
> To quit the house at morning's prime,
> At six or so, about the time
> When watchmen, conscious of the day,
> Puff out their lanthorn's rushlight ray.
> . . . .

> Tis Life, to reach the livery stable
> Secure the *ribbons* and the day-bill
> And mount a gig that had a spring
> Some summers back . . .
> Tis Life to revel down the road
> And *queer* each o'er fraught chaise's load;
> To rave and rattle at the *gate*
> And shower upon the gatherer's fate
> Damns by the dozen, and such speeches
> As well betoken one's slang riches
> To take of Deady's bright stark naked
> A glass or so—'tis LIFE to take it
> To see the Hurst with tents encampt on.
> Etc, etc.

Sporting enough! But Reynolds reached Moulsey in comparative comfort while Tom, Sam and Billy, three Tothill fanciers, were not so lucky:

> The Watchman was crying 'past four',
> When lanky Tom Lenny arose;
> He jumped out o' bed on the floor,
> And groped in the dark for his clothes.
> Him, cross-eyed Billy Smart,
> And Sam Grope had agreed over night
> And borrowed Aby Long's horse and cart
> To go down and see the fight.

They exchanged civilities with the turnpike keeper and

> guv'd him a bad half-crown
> 'Twas so dark that he could not see
> And, though the rain still pattered down,
> They started again off with glee.

However, they were on the wrong road and had to be directed to Moulsey.

> The mare again put in the cart,
> 'Cross the country to Moulsey to roam,
> But not liking that way to start,
> She bolted straight forwards for home,
> She ran as if drove by a witch

Tom Lenny held the reins tight;
She capsized them all in a ditch,
Going to see the fight.

Tom Lenny got out of it first,
And all round about him did stare;
Sam Grope swore, bellowed and curs'd,
And Bill Smart he walloped the mare.

They had to refund Aby Long a matter of £5 or £6 for repairs to his cart and they never got to the fight. The moral of the story holds good to this day.

Never choose a man with cross sight
Nor get out of bed backside first,
When you're going to see a fight.

Both with gentlemen and costermongers the public houses were thronged to excess at a fight and a large '*dollop of blunt* was got rid of in the *peck and booze* way'. The Fancy enjoyed a healthy thirst and appetite. At North Walsham after Painter fought Oliver, 'the place was literally drained of every article it possessed in the eating line in the course of an hour or two; and as to Hollands, Rum, Brandy and Wine, the rapid demand for all these renovators of the constitution . . . beggared all description'. On tour, the Fancy were accustomed 'to drop their *blunt* like waste paper; and no questions asked'.

Apart from their Metropolitan manners and their attachment to the game the Fancy were distinguished by their dress and their speech. Hazlitt describes the dress as a 'double portion of great coats, clogs and overhauls'. The superfluity of clothing was of inestimable value in travelling in winter or standing round a prizering, but it was also a sort of uniform which members were pleased to wear. Reynolds describes it thus:

. . . a large drab coat
With large pearl buttons all afloat
Upon the waves of plush— . . .
A kerchief of the King cap dye

> (White spotted with a small bird's eye)
> Around the neck—and from the nape
> . . . an easy fanlike cape.

The headgear varied from the slouched hat of Bill Gibbons to the stovepipe of Pierce Egan and the beaver of the Corinthian Fanciers. Tom Owen decorated his 'upper-works' with a white topper and for a time white toppers became quite the 'go'. It was at this time that 'Orator' Hunt sported a white top hat and it was recognised as a symbol of radical beliefs. There were conservative men who believed that trousers and turned-down collars encouraged fast talk and slang.

As the Fancy had their uniform so they had their passwords, their language. In *Tales of a Traveller* Geoffrey Crayon (a pseudonym of the American Washington Irving) says: 'What is the slang language of the Fancy, but a jargon by which fools and knaves commune and understand each other, and enjoy a kind of superiority over the uninitiated?' There is some justice in his observation, for it was often convenient for the Fancy to communicate and at the same time exclude a 'joskin' (countryman) from their conversation. It was the speech of the tic-tac man, an urgent communication of the odds on which the livelihood of many depended.

In this chapter I have quoted extensively from the 'slang-whang' writers to give some idea of the Fancy slang. In brief, the Fancy's language was a combination of sporting technicalities and cockney and underworld slang. We have seen Reynolds' description of the gentlemen using 'such speeches as well betoken one's slang riches' and 'Paul Pry' explaining that the Fancy invariably seemed to finish their sentences with 'I'll bet you two to one'. In fact, the Fancy's language could quickly be learnt by anyone interested enough in their pursuits. To those not interested, the Fancy could reason that ignorance was bliss. The language was, of course, given the widest currency in the works of Egan and Bee, and *Bell's Life* in its sporting pages used it almost exclusively. It was picturesque and had the comfortable security of the old and well loved joke; and it could be excessively tedious. The significance of the association of Fancy language with cant or the language of the underworld has an altogether different significance, which I shall discuss at the end of this chapter.*

We have followed the Fancy down the road to Moulsey and to North Walsham; now we must meet them on their home ground in London. The temples of the Fancy were the sporting houses, the public houses kept by pugilists or by landlords providing the entertainment of the Fancy sports. Here the Fancy would gather to discuss the last contest and the likely issue of the next; matches would be made, deposits put down and the odds quoted. Every evening would certainly end with a 'chaunt', in which these sportsmen delighted. Egan's ability to provide doggerel ballads on recent sporting events made him a popular chairman at such evenings and have helped obscure his genuine literary talents in other spheres. A typical tavern chaunt of Egan's was the 'Castle Tavern':

> Well stored is our CASTLE, a long seige to stand,
> To *parley* or *fight*, we can all take a *hand*;
> Like trumps stick together, afraid of no plot,
> But beware of being *floored* by TOMMY'S grape *shot*!
> To banish dull Care, or to roar out a *Catch*,
> Take part in a GLEE, or, making a MATCH,
> Chaunt the pleasures of Sporting—the charms of a Race,
> And ne-er be at *fault*—at a MILL, or the Chase!

> Then let us be merry,
> While drinking our Sherry,
> For friendship and harmony can't last too long,
> Be still our endeavour,
> That nothing shall sever,
> The LADS OF THE FANCY at the Castle so strong.

* I have not attempted a glossary of the 'Fancy' language quoted in this chapter. Often in 'literary' slang the words are intended to make a visual or aural impact, their meaning being secondary. Those interested in translations might start with Mr Partridge's 'Dictionary of Slang'.

If the temples of the Fancy were the public houses then the nectar of the Fancy was assuredly 'daffy'. It was also known as *Old Tom, blue ruin, white tape, max* or *geneva*; it was *Jacky*, or *stark naked, Fuller's earth* or a *flash of lightning*. In short it was GIN. And it gave its name to the most famous of the assemblies of the Fancy. But as Egan says:

> To have denominated this Sporting Society the 'GIN CLUB' would not only have proved barbarous to the ear, but the vulgarity of the chaunt would have deprived it of many of its elegant friends. It is a subject, however, which must be admitted has a good deal of *Taste* belonging to it—and as a sporting man would be *nothing* if he was not *flash*, the DAFFY CLUB meet under the above title.

The Daffy Club was established at the Castle Tavern, Holborn, shortly after Tom Belcher had taken over the licence in 1814. It was in many ways a low-life version of the Pugilistic Club formed at the same date. Members of the Daffy Club were not well breeched enough to provide purses to be fought for, but in every other way they endeavoured to promote the sport of boxing. Tom Belcher remained landlord of the Castle until 1828 and it was in 1824 that *The English Spy* paid a visit to the Daffy Club and gave the following description (see p 151):

> The long room is neatly fitted up and lighted with gas; and the numerous sporting subjects, elegantly framed and glazed, have rather an imposing effect upon the entrance of the visitor, and among which may be recognised animated likenesses of the late revered Jem Belcher, and his daring competitor (that inordinate *glutton*) Burke. The fine whole length portrait of Mr. Jackson stands between those of the Champion and Jem Belcher; the father of the present race of boxers, old Joe Ward, the Jewish phenomenon, Dutch Sam; Bob Gregson in water colours, by the late John Emery of Covent Garden Theatre; the scientific contest between Humphreys and Mendoza; also the battle between Crib and Molyneux; portraits of Gulley, Randall, Harmer, Turner, Painter, Tom Owen and Scroggins, with a variety of other subjects connected with the turf, chase, etc., including a good likeness of the dog Trusty, the champion of the canine race in 50 battles,

and the favourite animal of Jem Belcher, the gift of Lord Camelford—the whole forming a characteristic trait of the sporting
world. The long table, or the *ring*, as it is facetiously termed, is
where the *old standers* generally *perch* themselves to receive the
visits of the *swells*, and give each other the *office* relative to
passing events. And what set of men are better able to speak of
society, in all its various ramifications, from the cabinet-counsellor
to the *cosey costermongers*?

This was indeed the top table of the Fancy. The President of
the Daffies was Jemmy Soares. By profession a sheriff's repre-
sentative, or bum-bailiff, Jemmy was 'as good a fellow as ever
tapped a *shy one* on the *shoulder joint*, or let fly a *ca sa* at your
goods and chattels'. Jemmy was no gentleman, but he was an
original of nature, and a favourite subject for the pen of Robert
Cruikshank, appearing in at least three of that artist's paintings.

Other leading lights were Pierce Egan himself, 'an eccentric in
his way, both in manner and in person, but not deficient in that
peculiar species of wit which fits him for the high office of
historian of the ring'. Other regulars included Adey the Greek,
Lucky Bob, and Di the table-lifter, a man who could bend iron
bars but had no stomach for a fight. Caleb Baldwin, too poor to
be a regular in Tom Belcher's parlour, was one of the completest
Fanciers—an echo of old Bill Gibbons. Caleb was so devoted to
the fancy sports that he wanted to know if there was any law
against 'cat-fighting', as he had a Tom he was prepared to match
against any cat in Christendom.

A fascinating footnote to the Castle Tavern's activities came in
1835 when Branwell Brontë, provided by his aunt with money to
join the Royal Academy Schools, returned to Haworth after a few
days, having dissipated his funds at Tom Spring's hostelry.

The more intelligent members of the Fancy were often little
more than men with an air 'of that knowledge of the world and
captivating freedom of manner, which is to be acquired in public-
house parlours, and at low billiard tables'. Intelligence, in this
context, can better be described as low cunning, of which the

Fancy was never short. In matters of the Fancy, a Rawdon Crawley could often outwit his intellectual superiors.

There were men like Gully, with phenomenal memories for figures or sporting performances. The Fancy, however, remained too easily convinced, like Tony Weller, that 'the man as can form a ackerate judgment of a animal can form a ackerate judgment of anythin' '. Gully, of course, was the exception rather than the rule.

Dickens 'Out-and-out young gentleman' synthesised some of the predictable characteristics of the Fancy. He drank rather a lot, smoked at all hours, and 'swore considerably'. He was happiest in the company of his fellow out-and-outers where, alone, he seemed 'gentlemanly, clever, witty, intelligent, wise and well-bred'. He eschewed the company of respectable women, who, quite reasonably, found the most favourable thing that could be said about him was that he was an 'eccentric person, and rather too wild'. This, he would take to be a compliment. Monty Darty and George Forsyte from *The Forsyte Saga* were latter-day Fanciers. Many of the bucks in Fancy Society turned out to be clerks or apprentices, 'released from a counter to act the gentleman, and cut a swell for a few hours at night'.

There were indeed some few men of intelligence and wider abilities among the Fancy, men like Pierce Egan, Vincent Dowling, and Jack Emery, a comic actor who wrote witty couplets and who was an able watercolourist. George Kent, a writer on the staff of the *Weekly Dispatch*, was an amusing conversationalist when sober, and something of an oracle in Fancy circles.

But excluding the gentlemen and literary fanciers, who were visitors to the Fancy's world, the general run of the Fancy were insensitive and crude. Sympathy they might have, but sensibility never. The following anecdote, taken from the *Sporting Magazine* of 1796, will serve to illustrate the point. A large crowd is watching a turn-up between a coachman and a publican:

> At length the coachman fixed a vigorous blow under the ear of his adversary . . . and left him sprawling on the ground in a most deplorable condition. . . .

Yet this sad plight seemed to obtain very little attention from
the spectators, the greatest part of whom bore off the victor in
triumph, and accompanied him to the public house.

Gentlemen fanciers might on occasion turn away from a bloody
battle, but a true fancier never.

There is no doubt that the Fancy included many undesirable
characters who worked to corrupt the sport to their own advantage. Egan usually chose to ignore such men, and Bee's frothing
indignation against those who fixed fights is difficult to evaluate
as evidence. *Bell's Life*, describing the change of administration
in the Fancy when Bill Gibbons retired, tells how Jack Scroggins
went to explain things to the leaders of the 'prigs' (thieves) and
'made it *allright* over a couple of gallons of heavy wet'.

More serious charges still were laid against the Fancy by
contemporary observers. Geoffrey Crayon (Washington Irving)
wrote:

> What is the Fancy itself but a chain of easy communication,
> extending down from the peer to the pick-pocket, through the
> medium of which a man of rank may find that he has shaken hands
> at three removes, with the murderer on the gibbet.

This was nearer to the truth than the writer can have imagined,
as the career of John Thurtell, executed for murder in 1824, was
to show. After Thurtell's execution, Pierce Egan published an
account of the trial, together with details of two interviews he had
with the murderer after his trial, and Egan added his recollections
of Thurtell as a member of the sporting world.

Thurtell had been a bombasin manufacturer in Norwich but
had gone bankrupt. It seems probable that he cheated his credi-
tors by claiming he was robbed of the proceeds of the sale of his
remaining stock. Moving to London he started in business again,
but his premises were burnt down, and he was charged with
intent to defraud the insurance company of £20,000. He was
fortunate in being acquitted, but he was now well established on
the road which was to lead him to the gallows.

On the failure of his second business venture he became a

full-time member of the sporting fraternity, earning a precarious living on the fringes of the world of the prizefighters. Hazlitt describes talking to him on the Mail to Newbury, and calls him a 'trainer'; he had indeed helped the 'Gasman' to train, and he seconded Jack Martin in at least one of his fights with Jack Randall. He had also helped promote the fight between Painter and Oliver in his native Norwich in 1820, and on one occasion he posed as Jack Martin in a provincial sparring tour, a typically dishonest touch.

But these activities did not bring in an income large enough to satisfy Thurtell, and he endeavoured to supplement it by gambling. As a gambler, however, 'he had not the talents to win, without his *luck* was ready made'. 'In some instances', says Egan, 'his character was not exactly free from such an imputation.' Indeed he was accused by Aby Belasco of trying to persuade his brother Israel to throw a fight, and it seems likely that there were occasions when his blandishments were neither publicised nor unsuccessful.

By 1823, however, Thurtell was in serious financial difficulties and he robbed and killed one Mr Weare, a well known gambler. With two accomplices, Thurtell dragged the body through a hedge and concealed it in a pond. But one of the accomplices turned King's evidence, and Thurtell was tried, convicted and executed for a very squalid murder.

For a variety of reasons, however, the affair became a *cause célèbre*. Indeed, G. M. Trevelyan has said that the case created more popular interest than any other event between the Queen's Trial and the Reform Bill. Public interest in crime and criminals had reached an unprecedented peak, probably because of a large new mass of uneducated readers who were breaking their teeth on simple broadsheets. The *Newgate Calendar* had first been produced in 1773 but it was kept up to date in broadsheet lives of criminals, and in the early 1820s the *Observer, Weekly Dispatch, Bell's Life* and others featured crime reports as leading news stories.

There does not seem to be any striking reason why Thurtell's crime should have achieved its unique prominence in this mass of newsprint but Thackeray was to write in 1833:

> Light be the stones on Thurtell's bones—he was the best friend the penny-a-line men had for many a day. Corder (the murderer of Maria Marten in the Red Barn) was good . . . Burke (the body-snatcher) was good . . . many others were no doubt excellent —but John Thurtell was the flower of the flock.

It was, however, not only the penny-a-line men, among whom Thackeray would doubtless have included Egan, who wrote about Thurtell. Borrow and de Quincy were clearly fascinated by the man's deed, and Charles Lamb found himself quite unable to concentrate on the day of Thurtell's execution at Hereford.

Although his killing of Weare marked him out, Thurtell was very much a regular member of the Fancy. He had an interest in prizefighting, but he also saw a way to make money in the seedy and corrupt world in which the prizefights were set. Short of his final crime the career of Thurtell can be fairly taken as a paradigm of the lives of one section of the Fancy and there were members of the Fancy who would claim distinction because they had once shaken John Thurtell by the hand.

CHAPTER TEN

Pugilism in Print

The great period of pugilism coincided with a significant increase in the numbers of the English reading public. The popularity of prizefighting was undoubtedly stimulated by the reports appearing in the newspapers and by references to the sport in numbers of books and magazines. By a reciprocal process, the popularity of the sport made it newsworthy, and where at first pugilism was featured only as a curiosity, it came in a short time to claim a large amount of print.

In order to understand this process we must look briefly at the reading public. Reading was restricted, for the most part, to those who had received some sort of education, and until the late eighteenth century the educated classes formed only a small percentage of the population. Edmund Burke estimated that in 1789 the reading population numbered no more than 80,000, but in the next thirty years this figure was to increase dramatically. By the middle of the eighteenth century the Methodists were helping to stimulate literacy and the habit of reading. Although 'useful books' were the recommended reading, the Methodists did believe in its intrinsic value, and we need not doubt that they were numbered among the readers of the newspapers that sprang up in the last years of the century.

The principles of self-education inculcated by the Methodists were taken up by radical groups, but it was not only the self-educated who contributed to increased literacy, for the demands of a changing society, more complex in its machinery and organisation, began to put a premium on knowledge. From 1780 the Sunday schools played their part in fulfilling this hunger for education and by the 1790s a new reading public had been created, in which the lower classes represented perhaps a majority of literate people. Fears that this would create a revolutionary situation and partly in order to divert the appetites of the new readers from political food for thought, the Evangelicals poured a flood of cheap moral tracts on to the market at prices between ½d and 1½d a copy. In one year, 1795–6, the number sold reached the astonishing figure of 2,000,000. Reading was here to stay, and the demand was by no means restricted to political or moral material. Sport, and in particular prizefighting, featured in newspapers, magazines and in the 'sixpenny teachers' which poured on to the market in the last years of the eighteenth century.

The greatest volume of print on pugilism came, predictably enough, at the high point of the sport's popularity in the years on either side of 1820. The second volume of *Boxiana* appeared in 1818 and the third in 1821. Egan and Kent were writing for the *Weekly Dispatch*. *Bell's Life* was established in 1822. The *Sporting Magazine* continued with occasional comments on the sport and Jon Bee brought out *The Fancy Gazette* in January 1822 to succeed *The Fancy*. At the same time *Blackwood's* and the *New Monthly Magazine* were taking a more sophisticated, or certainly more literary, look at the sport.

In 1819 Tom Moore produced *Tom Cribb's Memorial to Congress* and in 1820 there appeared *The Fancy*, a series of poems by young J. H. Reynolds, perhaps the most interesting of all the literary contributions. In the same year pugilism was first featured in a series of books of which Egan's *Life in London* was the forerunner.

This was the high point of both the sport and its literature, but the first book about pugilism was probably Captain John Godfrey's *A Treatise upon the Science of Defence*, which was published in 1747. This work dealt mainly with swordplay, but devoted an illuminating chapter to pugilism. Godfrey tells us something of the heroes of the time and describes their techniques, and his work was much used by subsequent writers, as we shall see; it should be added that it was written by a gentleman for gentlemen.

The sport declined in the years following the publication of Godfrey's book, and, as we have seen, it was not until Tom Johnson became Champion in 1787 that widespread interest in the sport was revived. By this date both *The Times* and the *Morning Post* were established, and, more important, *The World* made its first appearance on 1 January 1787. The young Captain Topham was its founder, and the paper in its early days was under his general editorial direction. Topham was an influential figure in the newspaper world, and a remarkable figure in other spheres. Playwright, man of fashion, rake and sportsman, his much publicised mistress Mrs Wells, the well known actress, bore him three daughters before losing her reason. Topham retired to Yorkshire, his native county, in the same year, 1791, leaving his newspaper, and then lived the life of a literary sporting gentleman; but in the five years since 1787 he had established *The World* as the most fashionable newspaper of the day and he had set a number of precedents that were to be followed by other newspapers in the years to come. Apart from innovations in typeface and layout, the style of *The World*, which has been described as 'frivolous, up-to-date, and very personal', had its effect on its contemporaries and their successors.

The World is of particular interest with regard to pugilism for it was in its columns that there first appeared correspondence between two pugilists—Mendoza and Humphries. These open challenges were to become a feature of the *Weekly Dispatch*, then of *Bell's Life* and *Pierce Egan's Life in London and Sporting Guide*; but it was in the most fashionable and successful of newspapers, *The World*, that these pugilists' declamations were first featured. *The World* also carried occasional descriptions of prizefights, as in fact did the *Morning Post* and *The Times*, though *The Times* believed that prizefights were a national disgrace and ought to be prevented.

The rivalry of Humphries and Mendoza and the distinction of the sport's patrons had raised public interest to a new height and when the first edition of the *Sporting Magazine* appeared in October 1792 it began a 'History of Boxing', which it completed in five monthly instalments. This series would appear to be the first history of the sport, previous 6d publications having been concerned chiefly with its technique. The *Sporting Magazine* continued to report both major and minor provincial fights for the next forty years, until it came under the editorship of R. S. Surtees, who refused to cover such sports as prizefighting, cockfighting and baiting, and also, it is said, to employ Pierce Egan. The *Sporting Magazine* was written for the country gentry, and the *Gentleman's Magazine* and *Carlton House Magazine*, which also included articles and prints on pugilism, were read mainly by the traditionally educated middle and upper classes.

The new popularity of the sport, combined with a new reading public of uneducated and unsophisticated tastes, led to a flood of 'sixpenny teachers' on pugilism. Published in the last years of the eighteenth century, they were issued under the names of boxers —such favourites as Fewtrell, Mendoza, Joe Ward and Jem Belcher. In the *Annals of Sporting* in 1823 Jon Bee savagely reviewed the series, and on the grounds of literary merit his vituperation is entirely justified; but these 'ghosted' books, the first as far as I know to be written under the names of famous sportsmen, do have considerable interest. Each one drew freely on its predecessors, often only the alleged author being changed to keep up with the current favourites. The two earliest would

L

seem to be *The Art of Manual Defence; or System of Boxing*, and *Modern Manhood, the Art and Practice of English Boxing*. Both were published in 1788, the first written either by Captain Topham or by a barrister named Hall, and the second by an eccentric literary odd-job man called Harry Lemoine. Bee takes Topham (or Hall) as the prime originator, and believes Lemoine to be the plagiarist, but from what little we know of Lemoine he would seem to have been quite capable of putting together an original work on the level of *Modern Manhood*.

The merit of these books is that they fulfilled the demand of a newly literate but otherwise uneducated group. They were cheap, selling usually at 6d, longer lasting than a newspaper, and usually included an illustration, which contemporary newspapers did not. They were sold on hawkers' barrows or from the chapman's pack, together with books on crime and criminals, on magic and astrology, and with the gull's handbooks, which were a constant theme in cheap literature since the time of Ned Ward and earlier. For the most part these chapbooks are badly written and shoddily produced, but they remain, even to a modern reader, extremely attractive. What a marvellous alternative to Hannah More's *Moral Tracts* and the equally self-righteous fulminations of the political revolutionaries. Hannah had declaimed: 'The amusements of a Christian must have nothing in them to excite the passions . . . they must not . . . influence the lust of the flesh, lust of the eye and pride of life'. Pugilism was all that Hannah forswore and we may be sure that it proved more compelling to many of the newly literate than the new puritanism of the Evangelicals.

In 1811 came the publication of *Pancratia* by the comedian Bill Oxberry, which included a history of the sport, the first since the *Sporting Magazine*'s effort of 1792–3. Oxberry drew from the previous works, and in particular the newspaper reports.

The year 1812 saw the appearance of the most famous work of all—*Boxiana; or Sketches of Antient and Modern Pugilism, from the days of the Renowned Broughton and Slack to the Heroes of the*

Present Milling Aera. The work was dedicated to Captain Barclay and was published by and for G. Smeeton, 139 St Martin's Lane, London. The author chose to call himself 'One of the Fancy', and there remains an element of mystery regarding his identity. It is generally assumed to have been Pierce Egan, who at the time was a compositor in Smeeton's firm, and who undoubtedly was the author of volume 2 of *Boxiana*, published in 1818, and volume 3, published in 1821. Egan claimed to be the author of the original *Boxiana*, at first by implication but subsequently by specific statement. When volume 2 was published in 1818, the 1812 *Boxiana* was republished as volume 1 and the author was given as Pierce Egan; and *Blackwood's Magazine*, for example, took it that the question of authorship was resolved and that Egan was the sole author of the original work.

Jon Bee disputed Egan's claim in his *Dictionary of the Turf, the Ring, the Chase, the Pit, etc,* published in 1823, claiming that *Boxiana* of 1812 was written not by Pierce Egan but by Joseph Smeeton, who had stolen much from the work of Oxberry, which he claimed as his own. Bee then brings this tale to a moral conclusion by declaring that Smeeton did not profit from his dishonesty, dying in the fire which consumed his premises in the following year. Bee is never a reliable witness and he conducted a running feud with Egan, constantly attacking and denigrating the latter's achievements. He had more reason than usual, perhaps, in 1823 when his *Dictionary* appeared, because Egan, not for the first or the last time, had beaten him to the punch by producing his own *Dictionary* a few months previously. Apart from his jealousy of Egan, Bee's explanation of the authorship of the original *Boxiana* is clearly at fault in one particular: it has been established that Joseph Smeeton's house burned down in May 1809, long before *Pancratia* or *Boxiana* were published. The title page of *Boxiana* states clearly that it was published 'by and for G. Smeeton' (George, the nephew, not Joseph, the father).

It seems probable that Egan was the major contributor and certainly the editor of the original book, though it is possible that several hands assisted in collecting the material. It is significant, however, that George Smeeton, with whom Egan did not remain on the best of terms, never chose to dispute Egan's authorship, and as the publisher of the book, and himself a writer, he was in the best position to know. Another point in Egan's favour is that he was appointed sports writer to the *Weekly Dispatch* in 1816, two years before *Boxiana*, volume 2 and the reprint of the first volume under his name were published; and it is likely that he was appointed to the post in view of his contribution to the first volume, which was by then known to those connected with the sporting world. The work was initially published in parts, beginning on Friday, 17 July 1812 and ending on 1 May 1813. It was then published in one volume with the title page dated 1812.

In the book itself there is every indication of Egan's literary style. There was much use of slang but less of the picturesque analogy than was later to appear in his vast output. *Boxiana* was important because it gave pugilism, though not for the first time, the dignity of a detailed history. It drew together the threads of a story which had previously been disparate, and emphasised the social standing of the sport by describing the parts played in its promotion by the nobility and members of the middle classes. It provided amusement for the more sophisticated reader, who found pleasure in the anatomical impertinences essayed and the manner in which a blackguardly pursuit was claimed as a promoter of ethics, the safeguard of English liberties, etc.

The principal reason for the book's popularity was its character studies of pugilists, which revealed not only the fighting skills but the personal quirks of an unusual group of men. Before the publication of *Boxiana* the pugilists had rarely been seen as individuals, with the strengths and weaknesses of their physical and intellectual characters displayed. It was fascinating to learn of Jem Ward's predilection for paintings, of Bill Richmond's social graces, and of the ubiquitous Bill Gibbons, the asterisk to the world of the Fancy. *Boxiana* was the first book written for both the gentleman fancier and the lower-class members of that famous order. It became the standard work on the sport and established the history and the style of prizefighting.

Pierce Egan proved to be one of the outstanding journalists of the first quarter of the nineteenth century. His influence on early Victorian writers is only now being demonstrated. He was the natural successor to Ned Ward, the King of Grub Street in the early years of the previous century, since when Grub Street had produced no one with the style and imagination to influence his contemporaries on the higher slopes of literature. Like Ward, Egan was a literary hack writing to satisfy an immediate and unsophisticated demand and looking to an immediate financial return for his energies. But in pugilism the subject and the writer found themselves ideally complemented and Egan's imaginative approach helped to develop an entirely original, though highly imitable, style. Apart from his writings on pugilism Egan was to make major contributions to crime reporting, to the cult of the picaresque, to the development of the popular newspaper and to English usage, but he was first and last the chronicler of pugilism.

Born in London in 1774, the son of an Irish immigrant pavier, Pierce was apprenticed to a printer at the age of 12. His education in a formal academic sense was minimal. 'I tell you honestly,' he wrote at the end of his life, 'I am nothing else but a plain unlettered man.'

Nothing of his work as an author is known before the publication of *Boxiana* in 1812, though he may have helped in the compilation of some of the chapbooks published by Smeeton. In 1814 he wrote, printed and published a work called *Florizel and Perdita*, detailing the Regent's early infatuation with the actress Mary Robinson. Wisely, he was not to acknowledge authorship until 1843. In 1818 came volume 2 of *Boxiana*, taking the story of the sport from 1812 to that year. In 1818 he also produced a straightforward guidebook to the city of Bath, and in the following year he collaborated with Robert Cruikshank to produce an extraordinary work called *A Picture of the Fancy on the road to Moulsey Hurst*. Cruikshank designed the panorama 156in long by

2½in wide, which begins with the Fancy meeting in the Castle Tavern and in a series of brilliantly observed scenes follows the Fancy through Hyde Park down the road to Moulsey to witness a prizefight. After the fight there is a bullbait and the final scene takes place at Tattersall's on the following day, where settlement of the bets is made. This panorama, issued in pull-out roll form in a carved wooden box, was accompanied by Egan's text. No copy of the text is now extant, but extracts from it are quoted in newspaper advertisements and in Egan's other works. The panorama was still being sold in 1823, when it was advertised in the *Annals of Sporting*; it was another contribution to the familiarisation and glorification of the prizering.

Egan produced an unimportant memoir of George III in the year of that unfortunate monarch's death in 1820, but his name, which was now well known, was reversed to 'E. Pierce' on the title page. In the same year came a volume of *Sporting Anecdotes* and, more important, the first issues of *Life in London*, another collaboration between Egan and Robert Cruikshank. Issued in parts from August 1820, the work was an immediate success, with Egan's commentary aptly complementing the wit and in-genuity of the Cruikshank brothers' prints to tell the story of Corinthian Tom and his country cousin, the warmhearted Jerry Hawthorn. The two young men visit the sights of London, both among the high life and low life, and their visits take them to Gentleman John Jackson's Academy and Tom Cribb's tavern.

In 1821 *Life in London* was sold in a single volume at a price of 36s and it was a bestseller. It became a cult book, attracting a stream of imitators, and a number of adaptations were made for the stage.

Egan produced the third volume of *Boxiana* in 1821, a fourth in 1828 (parts had been issued from 1826) and a fifth in 1829. He also branched out as a newspaper proprietor with his *Pierce Egan's Life in London and Sporting Guide* and later, in 1829, *Pierce Egan's Weekly Courier to the Sporting, Theatrical, Literary and Fashionable World*. His *Finish to Life in London*, which brought a suitable moral end to Tom, Logic and Kate, included a visit to the public house kept by Pierce's friend Josh Hudson, the 'John Bull Fighter', but after 1829 he seems to have become less interested in boxing. Already he had set a new style of criminal reporting, with his famous death-cell interview with Thurtell, and his interest in the theatre, whetted of course by productions of *Life in London*, was beginning to lure him with a siren song. He became an actor himself and wrote a number of plays, including, perhaps predictably enough, *Life in Liverpool* and *Life in Dublin*. He produced a most interesting work in 1832 made up of 3d numbers and called *Pierce Egan's Book of Sports* in which No V, *Tom Spring's Parlour*, is compulsory reading for its picture of the Fancy's headquarters. Of course the sport had gone to the dogs, particularly the sport which Egan had been familiar with. Since 1824-5 the prizering had slid into a decline and Egan was well advised to pursue other interests. It is appropriate, though also a little sad, that towards the end of his life, in 1844, he was lecturing on the art of self-defence in Dublin, Edinburgh and Liverpool, and his last work, published in 1845 when he was 71, was entitled *Every Gentleman's Manual* or a *Lecture on the Art of Self Defence*. This is a delightful book, for the old man looks back on the sport he had quite certainly helped to shape. There are reminiscences of individual fighters and we learn, and this is virtually the only source, details of the fighters of the 1820s long after their ring careers are over. But it is clear that for Egan the sport had ceased before 1830, and that was in a different age.

Egan's *Life in London* had begun the rage for a series of picaresque episodic stories, including *Real Life in Ireland*, *Real Life in Paris* and two books in particular which included extremely interesting and well informed comment on the boxing world. These were *Real Life in London*, a work probably more successful than its inspiration, and a later work *The English Spy* by Basil Blackmantle (C. M. Westmacott). *Real Life*'s author is unknown, guesses range from Jon Bee to Henry Alken or 'old' Combe (the author of the 'Syntax' verses). Both books, in their own way, boosted the image of the prizering as an interesting feature of the social background of the time.

Life in London contributed to the greater glory of pugilism and it was followed by the publication of three newspapers, two of which were to devote a great deal of space to prizefighting and which made their contribution to the development of the popular Sunday papers. In January 1822 William Macdonald brought out a Sunday paper called by the very name of Egan's work, *Life in London*. Then in March 1822 Robert Bell brought out *Bell's Life in London*, which quickly incorporated Macdonald's paper. Egan was at this time still working for the *Weekly Dispatch*, but in January 1824 he was dismissed, yet brought out his own paper less than a fortnight later, a remarkable feat of organisation. The new paper was called *Pierce Egan's Life in London and Sporting Guide* and sold at 8½d, the same price as the bigger *Weekly Dispatch*, and 1½d more than its direct competitor *Bell's Life in London*, or *Bell's Life* as it is usually known.

From 1 February 1824 there were then three weekly papers devoting considerable space to reports on the matchmaking, the fights, the sparring benefits and sundry ring affairs. *The Weekly Dispatch*, a mildly radical paper, had carried the writings of Pierce Egan from 1816 until January 1824, when George Kent took over. *Bell's Life* was short on politics but it was long on crime reports and ring affairs under the editorship of Vincent Dowling, with 'Frosty-faced Fogo' the poet in residence. *Pierce Egan's Life in London* featured Pierce himself as the principal writer on ring affairs. The quality of journalism was high, for Kent, Dowling and Egan had considerable talent.

George Kent was a witty and well informed writer and himself a sparrer with the pugilists. Egan described him as a sort of *oracle* to Bob Gregson, 'the word and opinions of Mr. Kent were, in the eyes of the Lancashire hero, completely orthodox'. Attractive though he was to the pugilists, deficiencies in his character rendered him less popular among the theatre owners, publicans and watchmen, 'his fame for a spree' being 'perfectly established at the Police Offices'. George drank too much too often and not only his temper suffered, so did his concentration. Egan, himself the most persistent of scribes, said sadly: 'He commenced three or four sporting publications connected with the boxers, but he never completed any of them'. It is my own view that Egan put some of his friend George Kent as well as himself into the character of that attractive and irresponsible Oxonian, Bob Logic.

While Kent was unable to sustain his creative energies Vincent Dowling was noted for an industry that never tired. He was the editor of, and a principal contributor to, *Bell's Life in London* for nearly thirty years from 1822. A tall gentlemanly-looking man with spectacles, Dowling was both generous and honest, his incorruptibility a byword in Fancy circles. Egan, whose generosity to his rivals does him credit, says: 'no man, in his literary capacity, has afforded greater amusement to the public, than Mr. Dowling'. In his social hours Dowling could unbend, and enjoyed above all to recite 'An Irish Tale'.

For some years Dowling employed the poet laureate of the prizering, Frosty-faced Jack Fogo, who contributed some genuinely witty poems to the pages of *Bell's Life*. His nickname described his pockmarked visage and the one-time tailor became a popular figure in the sporting world and in great demand to compose and chaunt his ditties at the boozing dens of the Fancy as well as in the columns of their favourite newspaper. The prizering produced a number of poets, but apart from the contributions of literary outsiders like Christopher North, J. H. Reynolds and Tom Moore, only Fogo has any claim to merit. His style would suit the declamations of Stanley Holloway, and it was no doubt with something of a lugubrious sepulchral style that Fogo himself delivered them. His style was a mixture of puns, slang and pedantic literary allusions.

Fogo usually had a strong story line. Here Ben Burns, a former pugilist, and now promoting the ring claims of his nephew Jem, has challenged Fogo for the title of poet laureate of the ring:

With all my heart (said Fogo). I'm content
Whoever's *Champion*: 'tis an honour lent
Until a better claimant takes the field
And makes the former Champion say 'I yield'.
I'm but the Poet Laureate of the Ring
Who'er is Champion or who'er is King.
Cried Ben, 'You Poet!—Poetry's all lies:
I can write better—if not, d——n my ——'
'As far as lying goes, and all men know it',
Jack Randall said, 'You'd make a first-rate poet'.
Now Uncle Ben did not approve this jest,
When followed by a laugh from all the rest
Who sat at table: 'twas a full flush bit
And had, what's worse, as much of *truth* as *wit*.
He flew into a passion—never greater;
But what he said required a good translator.
However in the end when he was cool
And had restrained his tongue within some rule,
He challenged Fogo, that 'ere Wednesday night,
That each a specimen, or prize should write
For just a dozen of good bottled ale.
The articles were drawn—should either fail,
The other was to pay, and they might choose
The subject they thought fitted for their Muse.
They both are at it now: in next week's paper
We'll publish these effusions of their vapour.
Each man is confident, that he shall win;
And Ben Burns, to avoid domestic din,
Has shut himself within a garret high
For poets love the first floor from the sky,
At least 'tis that they chiefly occupy.

Rhyme, if not poetry, has a peculiar fascination for the under-educated, the rhyme itself being taken as a signal of learning and even of wit, and some dreadful doggerel was acclaimed by the Fancy. Egan was responsible for some of it, his talent for poetry being minimal, though it is only fair to say that most of his verse was meant to be sung and lyrics can look extremely poor on paper. Bob Gregson, who had fought Cribb and Gully, was thought to have a talent for poetry. The following is a fair example of his style:

> When RANDALL leap'd into the ring,
> He threw up his hat so gaily, O!
> And taking TURNER by the hand,
> He shook it frank and freely, O!
> Each man then stripp'd and took their view
> Which way was the best to handle, O!
> When the lads sung out from St. Giles's troop,
> What a 'broth of a boy' is JACK RANDALL, O!

There was some particularly amusing poetry written by the literary men. Although intelligent men could write about pugilism in prose in serious vein, if they turned to poetry it was almost invariably in lighter vein.

Tom Moore wrote *Tom Cribb's Memorial to Congress*, in fact a political caricature directed at the Prince Regent, and the reactionary rule of monarchs inspired by their belief in the divine right of kings. Moore said he wrote it because 'I flatter myself it serves the cause of politics which I espouse'. Gillray could have been more succinct and ruthlessly efficient, but Moore's poem is of interest because he chose to express himself like a number of graphic caricaturists, in the metaphor of boxing. Moore in fact was not a fan of boxing, and it was his wish to write a poem in the 'flash' language rather than any desire to glorify pugilism. His friends Byron and Scrope Davis were the devotees of the sport, and he accompanied Scrope to the Randall–Turner fight in December 1818 in order to gain material for the 'flash' poem. He found the fight 'not so horrid as I expected', though 'Turner's face was a good deal dehumanised'. He composed much of the poem lying in bed, his favourite position for composition, and produced it without any significant birth pains. 'This sort of stuff goes glibly from the pen. I sometimes ask myself why I write it . . . at all events it brings a little money without much trouble.' He himself did not particularly like it and though it was serialised in the *Morning Chronicle* and republished by Egan in his *Sporting*

Anecdotes of 1820 to an admiring audience of sports fans it was not a particular success. 'Cribb is not happy,' his publisher Murray succinctly advised him.

John Keats told Mr and Mrs George Keats there was 'nothing in it' and Mary Russell Mitford took an equally poor view of the poem; and as for Egan's readers, and perhaps Egan himself, the poem was not appreciated for what Moore had intended it to be. Moore was right in believing it a *coup manqué*, too vulgar a subject perhaps for refined readers, and too refinedly executed for the vulgar ones.

From the time of the publication of Moore's poem a number of witty poems were published on the subject of boxing. First came Christopher North, the pen name of Professor John Wilson of the University of Edinburgh and editor of *Blackwood's Magazine*. Wilson had been an athlete of note in his Oxford days and he retained a fondness for sports, delighting in particular in the incongruity of treating pugilism as a serious matter. From 1818 he had serialised *Boxiana* with his own praise of the virtues of Egan as a historian, but he produced his masterpiece of irony on the sport when, in May 1820, he published a *Luctus on the Death of Sir Daniel Donnelly, Late Champion of Ireland*. Wilson records the supposed tributes received from scholars, in Greek, in Hebrew, and in Latin:

> Anglorum nunquam cohortem magnanimus in pugna tristi
> Pugilum timuisti (heu ter lugende DONELLE!)
> Sed si quis te val Hallus, vel Olivarius in creparet,
> Vel Coöperus (heu!! etc)

Mr W[illiam] W[ordsworth] contributed an extract from his great autobiographical poem:

> Yea, even I,
> Albeit, who never 'ruffian'd' in the ring,
> Nor know of 'challenge', save the echoing hills;
> Nor 'fibbing' save that poesy doth feign;
> Nor heard his fame, but as the mutterings
> Of clouds contentious on Helvellyn's side,

Distant, yet deep, aguise a strange regret,
And mourn Donnelly—Honourable Sir Daniel:
(Blessings be on them, and eternal praise,
The Knighter and the knighted):* Love doth dwell
Here in these solitudes, and on corporal clay,
Doth for its season bear the self-same fire,
Impregnate with the same humanities,
Moulded and mixed, like others. . . .

B[yron] sent from Venice the commencement of a new poem
'Child Daniel', which includes:

What boots t'inquire?—'tis done. Green mantled Erin
May weep her hopes of milling sway past by,
And Crib, sublime, no lowlier rival fearing,
Repose, sole Ammon of the fistic sky,
Conceited, quaffing his blue ruin high,
Till comes the Swell, that come to all men must,
By whose foul blows Sir Daniel low doth lie,
Summons the Champion to resign his trust,
And mingles his with Kings, Slaves, Chieftains, Beggars' dust!

Wilson proposed an epitaph for Donnelly's tomb which included the following lines, referring to Dan's predilection for
potheen as well as pugilism:

O'erthrown by punch, unharmed by fist,
He died unbeaten pugilist!

Wilson had been praising Egan with a fairly friendly irony for
some years, and Pierce, as Westmacott pointed out, had the good
sense to take *Blackwood's* praise quite literally. On the publication
of the *Luctus* Egan permitted himself a review of his critic's work.
'We do not understand the gist of them,' he said, but no doubt
'they are truly interesting'. He regretted not having the erudite
Bob Gregson to assist him but thought that with such acquaint-
ances as Bill Gibbons and Daniel Mendoza he might possibly be
apprised of the meaning of the [St Giles] Greek and the Hebrew.

In this same year, 1820, a young poet named J. H. Reynolds

* The Regent and Dan Donnelly.

published a book of poems called *The Fancy*. Reynolds, a friend of Keats, had made his mark in the literary world with a number of parodies of Wordsworth and others, and it was the more surprising that he gave up poetry to become a solicitor, though he contributed work to the literary magazines, including occasional sporting subjects. But before he became a prose-writing solicitor he completed a series of poems with a background of pugilism. They are varied in mood.

> I've watched the bruiser's winning art,
> To lure his friend into his arms,
> And punch his head with all his heart,
> Commingling all the face's charms:
> I've watched the seconds pat and nurse
> Their man; and seen him put to bed;
> With twenty guineas in his purse,
> And not an eye within his head.
>
> ('King Tims the First')

> Bessy the beautiful, you needs must think,
> Was not without her feelings or her suitors:
> She was adored by those who are the pink
> Of that wild neighbourhood—by college tutors
> And sober serjeants. . . .

> The highest in the Fancy—all the game ones
> Who were not very much beneath her weight
> Would take her ivory fingers in their lame ones
> And woo her very ardently to mate:
> But she, although she did not love the tame ones,
> Was not for men of such a desperate fate;
> She knew a smart blow, from a handsome giver,
> Could darken *lights* and much abuse the *liver*.

> And eyes are things that may be bung'd or blackened—
> And noses may lie down upon the face—
> Unless the pace of a quick fist is slackened;
> And jawbones will break down, to their disgrace;
> And oftentimes a facer from on the back hand
> Will leave of poor humanity no trace.

She, like a prudent woman, well reflected
On all these things, and dozens she rejected.
('The Fields of Tothill')

Reynolds published no more pugilistic poetry after *The Fancy*, unless 'Bernard Breakwindow' was one of his several pen names. 'Breakwindow' wrote some pleasantly literate poetry under the titles of *Jack Randall's Diary* and *Randall's Scrap-book*. 'The best of the lot', pronounced Jon Bee, 'both contain various pleasing "jeux d'esprits" concerning several men in the ring, which were well hit off.'

The publication in 1822 of the first volume of the *Annals of Sporting and Fancy Gazette* brings forward the name of Jon Bee, a prolific hack who played a considerable part in the chronicling of pugilism. It is unfortunate that many of Bee's statements can be seen to be manifestly untrue, so that there is a danger of ignoring the genuine contribution to a full understanding of the sport which Bee's various works can provide. His life and times deserve more examination than has been applied to them and there are huge gaps in the story. What we know of his works is of great interest. Bee's real name was John Badcock (JB) and he wrote under a number of pen names in addition to the Jon Bee by which he is best known. He was a literary hack, and like other hacks he thought himself to be deprived of fame and riches by the perversity of publishers, fellow writers and the ignorance of the public. He had that 'little learning' which is most dangerous, and his jealousy of the uneducated but successful Egan is a constant motif in his writing. For one who prided himself on his scholarship his performance was appalling; for if events did not occur he was quite prepared to invent them, while charging other writers with inaccuracies, falsehoods and all. He had the qualities of mind which make, and more often break, would-be encyclopaedia makers, believing his own unconcentrated magpie-like mind to be that of a great scholar.

In his compositions his research was plagiarism, his insights often invention and his sympathies frequently the kiss of death.

He could never have written *Real Life in London*, which some later critics have ascribed to him; it is a work of greater humour and sympathy than Bee could ever have aspired to. But Bee's writing on prizefighting is valuable.

He began a magazine called *The Fancy*, which ran for six months, and in January 1822 published the first volume of *The Annals of Sporting and Fancy Gazette*, which was to rival the popularity of the old *Sporting Magazine*, which in fact bought Bee's magazine in June 1828. Without question Bee's most successful enterprise, *The Annals of Sporting*, was a monthly magazine 'entirely appropriated to Sporting subjects and Fancy Pursuits' and the *Fancy Gazette* was that section of the magazine dealing with the prizering—giving reports on recent fights and news of forthcoming fights, benefits and incidental items regarding the fighters. There is a strong impression that Bee was not an 'insider' as Egan undoubtedly was, but this enabled him to be more objective in recording the darker side of the world of pugilism.

By 1822 the sport was returning to the corruption that seems inevitable when the promoters come from the lower classes. Bee was alive to this—to the crossed fights and the artificial odds created by the London Fancy. He was contemptuous of the Londoners and was not afraid to publish the most swingeing criticisms in his monthly journal. He also forecast the end of the system of benefits which had proved so attractive and successful a feature of the prizering for twenty years. Bee pointed out again and again in the *Fancy Gazette* that fighters would kill the goose that had continued to lay the golden eggs if they abused the system by advertising star fighters who did not appear, and by refusing to help their fellow fighters by appearing at each other's benefits. It was Bee also who published the more scandalous details of the fighters' private lives and indicated that nobility of character was by no means the inevitable corollary of eminence in the prizering. Many fighters drank too freely to be able to restrain themselves from petty brutalities, and the generosity of

spirit which Borrow claimed for the bruisers of England was too
rarely observed by their intimates. Bee also wrote one volume of
Boxiana—volume 4, published in 1824—after Egan had quar-
relled with the publishers, Sherwood, Neely & Jones, after the
publication of volume 3. Bee's *Boxiana* is made up for the most
part of his pieces for the *Annals of Sporting and Fancy Gazette*,
but he performed his work well.

Perhaps Bee's most unusual work was his *Slang Dictionary of
the Turf, the Ring, the Chase, the Pit, of Bon-Ton, and the Varieties
of Life, forming the completest and most authentic Lexicon Bala-
tronicum hitherto offered to the notice of the Sporting World, for
elucidating words and phrases that are necessarily or purposely
cramp, mutative and unintelligible, outside their respective spheres.
Interspersed with Anecdotes, and Whimsies with Tart Quotations
and rum-ones; with examples, proofs and monitory precepts, useful
and proper for Novices, Flats and Yokels.* The work is as hysterical
and unbalanced as its title and Bee must almost certainly have
been mentally unstable when it was written. The encyclopaedia
mania had been the undoing of Thomas Sheraton, or at least a
manifestation of approaching insanity, and I do not think that
Bee's *Dictionary* can be understood without keeping this proba-
bility in mind.

I give below some few of Bee's definitions which maintain a
fine balance between spurious scholarship, vituperation, invention and interest. Any humour denoted therein may be assumed
to be unintended by the lexicographer.

BOX (verb)—to fight with the fists, but without science. As
pugilism is the highest kind of man-fight, so is boxing the lowest.
Several intermediate degrees of fighting capabilities are described
in the foregoing pages, of which *milling* and *hammering* are most
distinctly marked; the latter including those who slash away as if
they were mowing, and *wallop* their antagonists about the carcase
or *mow* (whence 'mow-wallop' and the term 'great walloping
chap' for a big country booby); the proceeding terms comprise
those who rush in roley, poley fashion, alike uncertain what is to
become of their blows. A 'boxing-bout' and 'boxing match' is

M

said properly of boy-fights or the contests of boobies, ploughmen, and navigators.

BOXOSOPHY—the philosophy of boxing, as exhibited monthly in the 'Annals of Sporting'.

GRUB-STREET—is applied to badly printed or ill composed writing, as the Weekly papers, 'Dispatch', & 'Advertiser'.

PUGILISM—the art and practice of manual defence. Derived from 'pugiles', the fists, and 'pugnandum', fighting; to throw the adversary when *in*, to get *out* from his clutches, or drop from his grasp, out of a chancery suit—are characteristics of the Bristol, or native school of pugilism.

SHAKING HANDS—the last ceremony preceding a well-regulated man-fight; and with some it marks the commencement of the battle, the shaking and thwacking having no interval.

The target was almost too easy for Professor Wilson in *Blackwood's*. He compliments Jon on his classical scholarship, quoting some of the more bizarre examples. 'In French Jon shines every whit as brilliantly, but we have not room to copy his specimens of what he might call Latincally the "Gallicus linguae".' Wilson was clearly fascinated by one aspect of life that Bee's book revealed—the variety of tavern-based clubs with which Bee appeared familiar. The 'Brilliants', the 'Eccentrics', the 'Finish', the 'Triponians' and the 'Rum-ones'. For the most part these were meetings of kindred spirits who, in the name of discussion, met to drink and chaunt. Their invitations to the 'Free and Easy' read 'N.B. Fighting allowed'. The existence and the customs of such clubs do not surprise us. It is my guess that they were more stimulated by the subject of prizefighting than by some of the half-baked revolutionary radical ideals they pretended to espouse.

The interest of Bee's writing is certainly not in its literary quality. We shall, however, close this chapter with a look at the finest piece of writing produced on the sport—Hazlitt's essay 'The Fight', first published in the literary *New Monthly Magazine* in February 1822 under the pen name of Phantases. Bee himself, typically, praised it and criticised it on different occasions. Just after its publication he wrote that it was 'the "ne sutor ultra crepidam" for a Scotch poet (which accounts for his observations) going to the Hungerford fight and scrawling eleven closely printed pages about it, (without a *scintilla* of *nous* in him)'. By 1824 he had complimented it!

'The Fight' is a splendid essay, an interesting tale with a moral, and gracefully written. It merits its place in anthologies for its style, but here it is the detailed observation that I wish to examine. I have quoted it several times in different contexts in this book and I believe it to be the most accurately observed and communicated piece of writing on the sport. The *ne plus ultra* not the *ne sutor ultra crepidam* of our classical friend.

Hazlitt takes us first to Jack Randall's public house to find out where the fight between Bill Neat and the 'Gasman', Tom Hickman, is to take place. The venues of fights, as we have seen, could not be advertised, but interested fanciers could find out from their local public house. Hazlitt was no regular fancier and he rather feared his reception from Jack Randall and his wife. He tells us much about the personal reputation of the 'Nonpareil' in the smallest vignette. Then there is the coach ride down to Newbury and the conversations with the trainer (Turtle or Thurtell). Hazlitt's description of the fight has a freshness which the regular reporters like Egan, Topham or Bee could never communicate. To the modern reader, as to Hazlitt, the whole business is extraordinary, and admiration for the courage of the principals is mixed with horror at the brutality of the sport and the unimaginative concentration of the Fancy. In a few pages Hazlitt has told us of the match-making, the venue, the travel, training and technique, the spectacle, the crowds, the characters of the fighters, and all in that flawlessly graceful style.

It says something, at least, for the impact which pugilism made on contemporary society, that it inspired one of the finest essays in the English language.

Envoi

Writing in his newspaper on 19 December 1824, Pierce Egan reported the meeting of Sharp and Reid at Moulsey Hurst:

> The fight, if it could be so termed, did not occupy more than three minutes, and to be dragged 16 miles from the Metropolis to witness such a representation of fighting was truly disgusting. But Milling may be said to be at an end; the Beaks will have little if any more trouble to interrupt it; and the Judges likewise have no further occasion to deprecate the system from the Bench. THE THING WILL STOP OF ITSELF. Who will make any more matches? Who will bet a single half penny after the display of Reid?

The same day in the *Weekly Dispatch* George Kent wrote:

> Alas the golden age of pugilism is gone. It cannot be denied that prize-fighting is on the decline . . . owing to the bad conduct of its professors. While some of them carry on in the same spirit of the olden time, others seem to be fond of 'X's'. At this period when a host of enemies are arrayed against the prize-ring, when the big-wigs are threatening, canting hypocrites are preaching, and many a scribe is dealing forth invective against milling and millers,—as if to assist these efforts, the Kingdom is divided against itself. If the real friends of pugilism do not exert themselves to put an end to *baulks* and *crosses* [thrown fights], the consequences must be fateful.

If such devotees as Kent and Egan were despondent it is clear that the sport was in danger. The rich upper-class patrons had withdrawn and promotion was in the hands of entrepreneurs and not gentlemen. The fighters had received too great a share of adulation and many seemed to have lost their self-respect. Dishonesty was as rife as in the bad days before Tom Johnson. Kent and Egan had suggested that the persecution of the magistrates would become more severe. They were proved right more quickly than they would have hoped.

Two days after their pieces had appeared in the press Ned Neale fought Jem Burns at Moulsey and a prosecution for breach of the peace at Kingston Assizes followed. Mr Justice Burrough declared prizefighting to be contrary to the laws of the country (well might *Bell's Life* call for 'Extermination to rotten *Burroughs!*'). He declared prizefights to be mercenary in origin and made up for the purpose of indulging the propensities of the vicious and encouraging the betting of the gamblers. His Lordship further expressed himself sorry to perceive that even those who have some pretension to the rank of gentleman are found to encourage them.

Bell's Life fulminated against the Judge and his judgement, but to no avail, for only one more fight took place at Moulsey Hurst, and the end of Moulsey precipitated the end of the prizering. Many more fights were to take place but it was never again to enjoy the wide measure of patronage it had enjoyed in its Regency heyday.

The obituary is by Vincent Dowling, writing in *Bell's Life* on 2 October 1825:

There is additional evidence of the decline, we might almost say fall, of the Fancy. The Corinthians . . . have ceased to grant either the light of their countenances, or the aid of their purses towards the encouragement of the Ring, and without such support, it is hardly necessary to note that prize-fighting can no longer have a local habitation or a name . . . when honour and fame cease to influence the combatants a system of low gambling is substituted. . . . We are not surprised that the Pugilistic Club, once so celebrated and so respected, (containing among its members some of the most distinguished individuals in the country) should have disappeared. It now unfortunately happens that the 'getting-up of Matches' is confined to classes which from circumstances, cannot be supposed to have either the means or the disposition to promote contests upon those patriotic principles on which the reflective part of mankind have hitherto been inclined to support them.

How has this come to pass? Why in the first instance it may be attributed to the absurd precedent which has been adopted in modern times, of backing second rate men for enormous stakes, and in the next, to the ingratitude which these men have shown to the people by whom they have been supported. 'Set a beggar on horse-back and he rides to the Devil'. So it is with many of the pugilists of the present day. They suddenly gain possession of a large sum, and are thus lifted into such imaginary consequence that they get above their business, and lose all recollection of the principle upon which they were supported. Fame and honour no longer form inducements to combat—nothing but 'filthy lucre' will now do, and thus the most sordid, or necessitous only are found to enter the lists. It was far different in times within the recollection of many living members of the Fancy, when the best men were found ready to enter the ring for £25 a-side, and to regard the pecuniary gain in a secondary point of view. The times may come again, but until they do, it will be difficult, if not impossible, to obtain the renewed countenance of the higher classes of society, who, in patronising prize fighting, do so rather from a desire to promote that manly spirit than to encourage a system of gambling and idleness.

Acknowledgements

I am grateful to three extremely busy people who took time to read the first draft of this book. Mr E. A. Smith, Senior Lecturer in History at the University of Reading, corrected a number of historical solecisms; if there are any present in the book they must have crept into the final draft. Dr M. Dorothy George exercised great patience with my enthusiasm for pugilistica and Eganiana and, from her comprehensive knowledge of the period, gave me a number of leads and a lot of inspiration. To Professor John Reid of the University of Auckland I owe a particular debt of gratitude; his researches into the details of Pierce Egan's life and his literary perception encouraged my own endeavours. I have been more fortunate in my preceptors than I deserve.

I also received valued assistance from members of the staff of the University of Reading Library, and Mrs Christine Bland and Mrs Ann Daish typed various drafts with high professional competence and informed interest. My wife prepared the index and the select book list, helped in innumerable other ways and sustained me during the long period over which this book was written.

Select Book List

NEWSPAPERS AND MAGAZINES
The Annals of Sporting and Fancy Gazette
Bell's Life in London and Sporting Chronicle
Blackwood's Magazine
The Globe
The Morning Post
The New Monthly Magazine
Pierce Egan's Life in London and Sporting Guide
Pierce Egan's Weekly Courier to the Sporting, Theatrical, Literary
    and Fashionable World
The Sporting Magazine
The Times
The Weekly Dispatch
The World

BOOKS
Abbey, J. R. *Life in England in aquatint and lithography* (1953)
Albemarle, Earl of. *Fifty years of my life*, 2 vol (1876)

Alken, H. T. *The national sports of Great Britain* (1820, reprinted 1903)

Altick, R. D. *The English common reader* (Chicago, 1957)

Amateur, An. *Real life in London*, 2 vol (1821)

Anon. *Corinthian parodies by Tom, Jerry and Logic* (1825)

—— *The Corinthian: an extensive collection of flash songs* (1830)

Apperley, C. J. ('Nimrod'). 'My life and times', ed by E. D. Cuming, *Blackwood's* (1927)

Bee, Jon, *pseud* [ie, John Badcock], ed. *The Annals of Sporting and Fancy Gazette* (1822–8)

—— *A slang dictionary of the turf, the ring, the chace, the pit, of bon ton, and . . . of the sporting world* (1823)

—— *Fancyana* (1824). Copy in John Johnson collection, Bodleian Library, Oxford

—— *Boxiana*, vol 4 (Sherwood, Neely, 1824). See also P. Egan. This volume also called *Bee's Boxiana*

Blackmantle, Bernard, *pseud* [ie, C. M. Westmacott]. *The English Spy*, 2 vols (1826)

Blaine, D. P. *An encyclopaedia of rural sports* (1858)

Borrow, G. *Lavengro* (1851)

—— *The Romany Rye* (1857)

Britton, J. *The original picture of London*, 27th ed (Longman, Rees, nd)

Buckley, G. B. *Fresh light on 18th century cricket* (1935)

—— *Fresh light on pre-Victorian cricket* (1937)

Butler, E. M. *A Regency visitor: the English tour of Prince Pückler-Muskau* (1957)

Byron, Lord. *Poetical works* (Oxford, 1967)

Chancellor, E. B. *Life in Regency and early Victorian times, 1800–1850* (1927)

Clare, John. *The prose of John Clare*, ed J. W. and A. Tibble (1951)

—— *The letters of John Clare*, ed J. W. and A Tibble (1951)

Cobbett, William. *Boxing* (1805)

Cook, Sir T. A. *A history of the English turf*, 3 vols (1901–[1904])

N

Creevy, Thomas. *The Creevy papers*, ed Sir H. Maxwell, 2 vols (1903)

Cuming, E. W. D. *British sport, past and present* (1909)

Darter, W. *Reminiscences of an Octogenarian* (Reading 1888)

Darwin, B. R. M. *John Gully and his times* (1935)

Dowling, Vincent. *Fistiana, or, The oracle of the ring* (1841)

Druid, The, *pseud* [ie, H. H. Dixon]. *Silk and scarlet* (1895)

—— *Scott and Sebright* (nd)

—— *Post and paddock* (nd)

—— *Saddle and sirloin* (nd)

Eardley-Wilmot, Sir J. E. *Reminiscences of the late Tom Assheton-Smith Esq* (1860)

Egan, Pierce. *Boxiana* (1812)

—— *Boxiana*, vol 2 (1818)

—— *Boxiana*, vol 3 (1821)

—— *New Series Boxiana*, vol 4 (1828)

—— *New Series Boxiana*, vol 5 (1829)

—— *Sporting anecdotes* (1820)

—— *Life in London* (1821)

—— *Finish to Life in London* (1828, reprinted 1887)

—— *Account of the trial of John Thurtell and Joseph Hunt* (1824)

—— *Recollections of John Thurtell* (1824)

—— *Book of sports* (1832)

—— *Every gentleman's manual* (1845)

Fitz-Barnard, L. *Fighting sports* (1921)

Fitzgerald, P. H. *The life of George IV*, 2 vols (1881)

Fulford, R. T. B. *George the Fourth* (1935)

—— *The Royal Dukes* (1933)

George IV. *Correspondence of George, Prince of Wales, 1770–1812*, ed A. Aspinall, 6 vols (1963–9)

Gaskell, C. M. G., ed. *An Eton boy: being the letters of James Milnes Gaskell, 1820–30* (1939)

George, M. Dorothy. *London life in the eighteenth century* (1925, 1966)

—— *Hogarth to Cruikshank: social change in graphic satire* (1967)
—— *Catalogue of prints and drawings in the British Museum: political and personal satires*, vols 5–11
Gilbey, Sir W. *Sport in the olden time* (1912)
—— and Cuming, E. W. D. *George Morland: his life and works* (1907)
Gittings, R. W. V. *John Keats* (1968)
Godfrey, Capt John. *A treatise upon the science of defence* (1747)
Grego, Joseph. *Rowlandson, the caricaturist*, 2 vols (1880)
Greville, C. C. F. *The Greville Diary*, ed P. W. Wilson, 2 vols (1900)
Gronow, Capt R. H. *Reminiscences and recollections of Captain Gronow, 1810–1860*, ed J. Grego, 2 vols (1900)
Grose, Francis. *A classical dictionary of the vulgar tongue*, ed with commentary by E. Partridge (3rd ed, 1963)
Haydon, B. R. *Diary of Benjamin Robert Haydon*, ed W. B. Pope, 5 vols (Harvard 1960, 1963)
Hazlitt, William. *The spirit of the age* (1825, 1969)
—— 'The Fight' (essay published in *New Monthly Magazine*)
Henning, F. W. J. 'Fights for the championship', 2 vols (*Licenced Victualler's Gazette*, 1902)
Hickey, W. *Memoirs of William Hickey*, ed P. Quennell (1960)
Hill, Draper. *Mr. Gillray, the caricaturist* (1965)
Huizinga, J. *Homo Ludens* (1949, 1970)
Hunt, Henry. *Memoirs of Henry Hunt, Esq.*, 3 vols (1820)
Lemoine, Harry, ed. *The Eccentric Magazine*, 2 vols (1812, 1813)
Lennox, Lord William Pitt. *My recollections from 1806 to 1873*, 2 vols (1874)
Liebling, A. J. *The sweet science* (1956)
Lillywhite, F. *Scores and biographies of celebrated cricketers*, ed A. Haygarth, vol I, 1746–1828 (1862)
Longford, Countess of. *Wellington: the years of the sword* (1969)
Lynch, Bohun. *The prize ring* (1925)
—— *Knuckles and gloves* (1922)

Melville, Lewis, *pseud* [ie, Lewis S. Benjamin]. *The beaux of the Regency*, 2 vols (1908)

Mendoza, Daniel. *Memoirs of the life of D. Mendoza* (1816)

—— *The art of boxing* (1792?)

Miles, C. D. H. *Pugilistica*, 3 vols (1880–1906)

Moore, T. *Poetical works of Thomas Moore* (1842)

—— *Life, letters and journals of Lord Byron* (1860)

—— *Memoirs, journal and correspondence of Thomas Moore*, ed Lord John Russell, 8 vols (1853–6)

Morison, Stanley. *Edward Topham, 1751–1820* (Cambridge 1933)

—— *The English newspaper, 1622–1932* (Cambridge 1932)

'Nimrod', see Apperley, C. J.

Nyren, John. *The young cricketer's tutor*

—— *The cricketers of my time*, ed C. C. Clarke (1833) with annotations by F. Ashley-Cooper (1902)

Osbaldeston, George. *Squire Osbaldeston: his autobiography*, ed E. W. D. Cuming (1926)

Piggott, Charles. *The Jockey Club* (1792)

Pycroft, J. *The cricket field* (1822, reprinted 1851)

Reid, J. R. *Bucks and Bruisers: Pierce Egan and Regency England* (1971)

Reynolds, J. H. *The Fancy: a selection from the poetical remains of the late Peter Corcoran* (1820)

Scott, J. R. *The history of cockfighting* (1963)

Shaw, G. B. *Cashel Byron's profession*

Slater, J. H. *Illustrated sporting books* (1899)

Smeeton, George. *Doings in London* (1828)

Smith, J. T. *A book for a rainy day* (1845, 1905)

—— *The streets of London* (1849)

Southey, Robert. *Letters from England by Don Manuel Alvarez Espiriella* (1807, 1951)

Squire, H. F. and A. P. *Pre-Victorian Sussex cricket* (1951)

Statnominisumbra, Esq. *The Battle of Barlborough* (MS dated 1807)

Tooley, R. V. *English books with coloured plates, 1790–1860* (1954)

Wheeler, C. A. *Sportascrapiana* (1867)

Windham, Rt Hon William. *The diary of Rt. Hon. William Windham, 1784 to 1810*, ed Mrs H. Baring (1866)

—— *The Windham papers, 1750–1810*, introd by Earl of Rosebery, 2 vols (1913)

Index

Figures in **bold** type indicate illustrations